D1550937

FROM THE LIBRARY OF

THE SHERATON DIRECTOR

THE SHERATON DIRECTOR

The furniture designs of Thomas Sheraton
arranged by

J. MUNRO BELL

Wordsworth Editions

This edition published 1990 by Wordsworth Editions Ltd,
8b East Street, Ware, Hertfordshire.

ISBN 1-85326-950-6

Printed and bound in Great Britain by Mackays of Chatham.

THOMAS SHERATON

1751-1804

IN Chippendale and Hepplewhite two types of master cabinet-makers and designers are exemplified. Both were practical craftsmen and successful business men. Robert Adam, the architect, and Thomas Sheraton the visionary, are representative of designers who influenced their contemporaries in a most remarkable degree, but who did not actually practise the art of cabinet-making themselves. (Sheraton abandoned practical work in 1793.) But here the comparison between Adam and Sheraton ends, for the former was the leading spirit in a great movement which had far-reaching effects in establishing a style which permeated architectural design and interior decoration and furniture. Robert Adam was eminently successful, but unfortunately Thomas Sheraton was one of life's failures, and died in poverty.

Born at Stockton-on-Tees in 1751, Sheraton describes himself as a "mechanic," in a religious pamphlet he published at Stockton in 1782. He came to London as a journeyman cabinet-maker in 1790, and after a few years he ceased working at the bench and occupied a small stationer's shop, where he was author, publisher, bookseller, teacher of drawing, and an occasional preacher at Baptist chapels. His character resembles that of William Blake, the painter, poet, and engraver, his contemporary. The successful Fuseli said of Blake's designs that they were "damned good to steal from," and there is little doubt that Sheraton's designs, published and unpublished, were a fine quarry for more practical men with greater aptitude for business. His own words convey a touch of his philosophic quality when he describes himself as "employed in racking my invention to design fine and pleasing cabinet-work. I can be well content to sit on a wooden bottom chair myself, provided I can but have common food and raiment wherewith to pass through life in peace."

It is the irony of fate that for the contemporary satin-wood furniture of Sheraton design, instinct with refined beauty, and graceful with a rare delicacy of invention, sensational prices are reached in the auction-room. Here again he touches William Blake, whose designs have won him eternal fame, but who often had not money enough when he lived to buy copper-plates to record his visions.

Another picture of the man Sheraton with his wife and two children has been given to posterity by Adam Black who, in 1804, came to London from Edinburgh in search of work. It was the year of Sheraton's death. Young Black found him "in an obscure street, his house, half shop half dwelling house, and looked himself like a worn-out Methodist minister, with threadbare black coat. I took tea with them one afternoon. There were a cup and saucer for the host, and another for his wife, and a little porringer for their daughter. The wife's cup and saucer were given to me, and she had to put up with a little porringer." The young Scotsman, afterwards publisher of the *Encyclopædia Britannica*, received half a guinea for his week's work in trying to bring arrangement into the ill-kept shop. "Miserable as the pay was," he writes, "I was half ashamed to take it from the poor man."[1]

Sheraton's first book of designs was issued in quarto parts, 1791-1794, "The Cabinet-Maker and Upholsterer's Drawing-Book." The complete volume is in three parts, together with an *Appendix* and an *Accompaniment*, containing a "variety of ornament adapted to the cabinet and chair branches." This consists of 113 plates of articles of furniture, sides of rooms, &c. The third edition of the *Drawing-Book* in four parts was published in 1802, and contains 122 plates, which edition is here republished. After Sheraton's death there appeared in 1812 a series of designs which Sheraton had in hand for publication. This "Designs for Household Furniture," with 84 plates "by the late T. Sheraton, Cabinet-Maker," is here republished.

The latter half of the eighteenth century from 1748, when Ince and Mayhew produced their volume with three hundred designs for *Household Furniture*, down to the death of Sheraton, was most prolific in the publication of illustrated books of design. The bibliography of the subject is full, and there is ample evidence that in the closing years of the century there was a complexity of theory. Styles of one maker were readily adapted by another, and published designs of men related to each other in details of construction, and deriving inspiration from a common source, overlapped in point of time. The number of master cabinet-makers, upholsterers, and chair-makers given by Sheraton as working in London and the vicinity was no less than 252. There is no doubt that many of these men did good work. What is known, for instance, of Seddon, "one of the most eminent cabinet-makers in London"? But according to the *Annual Register* of 1768 he had a fire at his premises in Aldersgate Street which did damage to the extent of £20,000.

The early Chippendale school had given place to the school of mar-

[1] "Memoirs of Adam Black," 1885.

queterie workers, compeers of Hepplewhite, who employed satin-wood veneer and inlays of coloured woods, and who revelled in painted panels with subjects as French in feeling as the lunettes of Natoire and Boucher. In 1773, so strongly had the current set in for colour, that Chippendale, then an old man, made a set of satin-wood furniture after the designs of Robert Adam for the Lascelles family. The beautiful contrasts of colour against the golden satin-wood ground are remarkable. The dressing-table commode of this suite has a veneered satin-wood ground inlaid with green garrya husks, and wreaths of this inlay encircle panels of seated figures of Diana and Minerva inlaid with coloured woods and ivory on a black ground. So elaborate were some of the pieces of this suite at Harewood House that the cast and chased metal work equals that of *Gouthière*.

Prior to Sheraton's day pieces of lesser magnificence than those executed for noblemen's mansions were painted in the Hepplewhite style, and the use of satin-wood was becoming popular. Sheraton came to London in 1790, and died in 1804, so that his influence as a designer extended only over a period of fourteen years. He found a rapidly increasing love for the elegance of the French designers, and he identified himself so much with boudoir art that many of his designs might well be taken as original French conceptions. The lathe is used more freely in Sheraton chairs and tables than by his forerunners. His details have a charm and delicacy unsurpassed in English design. In comparison with Hepplewhite he had a finely developed sense of proportion. Grace and symmetry are never wanting in his designs. He held very sound views in regard to ornament which in his work was never meaningless. It is part of the construction, and never appears to be an afterthought. It is reticent and subdued, but possesses a beauty which successive generations of connoisseurs have acclaimed.

The *Drawing-Book* tells its own story. The "Conversation Chairs" and Sofa (p. 3) require a word of explanation. The chairs were used by gentlemen who sat astride with the back of the chair facing the sofa, the seat of honour. The top of the chair was used for leaning upon. The backs for Parlour Chairs (p. 4) exhibit a rare delicacy of finely proportioned ornament. The delicacy of detail is exemplified in the Elbows for Drawing-Room Chairs (p. 7), and the Chair Legs (p. 8) indicate something more detailed in carving than is usually associated with Sheraton by collectors and students familiar only with the satin-wood examples of table legs of tapering form, with no carving, but dependent on inlay for their decoration. In the Card Tables and the Kidney Table (p. 13), one sees at once the touch of Sheraton. Chippendale would not have produced such a design as the kidney table with its novel form and its bowed fronts, and slender grace and elegance. Hepplewhite was too studied and painstaking to have conceived so original a design. Similarly in the borders for Pier Tables, Sheraton is as bold and original in his marqueterie design as was Chippendale in his carving in mahogany.

In regard to the elaborate mechanical devices in dressing tables and library furniture, it is possible that Shearer, who was a past master in such inventions, may have followed out these designs of Sheraton, and he probably had an influence on Sheraton in their conception.

The painted panel of the Hepplewhite school found its ideal in such examples as the Ornament for a Table (p. 14) with the fine figures of Venus and Adonis.

In regard to the painting of Sheraton's furniture by Angelica Kaufmann, there is room for considerable scepticism, as Sheraton did not come to London till 1790, and Angelica, on her marriage with Zucchi, left England in 1781, and resided in Rome till 1795.

A series of Bookcase Doors (pp. 20 and 21) exhibits Sheraton's originality of idea, and the leaves in carving show a grace and firmness of touch unapproached by Hepplewhite in his Prince of Wales's feathers.

The "Horse Dressing Glass" (p. 32) still retained in the word "Cheval" is merely a term denoting a larger size, made familiar in such phrases as horse-play, horse-laugh, horse-chestnut.

The Sideboard and Sideboard Table (p. 34) show graceful lines and curves not before introduced into English furniture, and essentially belonging to the school of designers founded by Sheraton.

In the *Designs for Household Furniture* the chairs depart in marked manner from the grace and symmetry of Sheraton's earlier forms. They mark his decadent period when he came under the influence of the Napoleonic modes in French furniture, and they betray, what is rare in Sheraton, a slight want of balance. Some of his Library Tables (notably that illustrated, p. 94) exhibit powerful design and well-balanced proportions.

As a summary of Sheraton's style, it may be advanced that he imparted to furniture a subtlety and elegance which broke away from the old traditions of the school of carvers. Robert Adam regarded furniture as an adjunct to his architectural details. He made the lines of his furniture designs subservient to the scheme of decoration. Away from its environment Adam furniture is hard and lacks repose. Sheraton designed furniture for the love of his art. His style is rich with piquant suggestiveness. In colour it is alluring, in form it is elegant and refined, and full of artistic surprises. The dainty boudoir was his by conquest. His furniture belongs to the age of the insipidities of the Bartolozzi school of stipple engraving, and to the finnicking mannerisms of the days of colour prints. His colour schemes found favour with Mrs Siddons, Mrs Fitzherbert, and Lady Hamilton. His importations from France, the pseudo-classicism of the court of Marie Antoinette, took root here as something new. But in spite of the source of his inspiration there is an originality of treatment which marks his style as distinctive, and stamps Sheraton as a master designer. There is much which may some day be discovered by research relating to firms such as Gillow and others, for whom Sheraton designed ; at present his work for contemporary cabinet-makers is lost in a crowded and prolific period. One is on sure ground when studying his published books of designs. Beyond this Sheraton's actual work is largely conjectural. But his influence in English furniture design is permanent.

THE CABINET-MAKER AND UPHOLSTERER'S DRAWING-BOOK.

IN FOUR PARTS.

BY

THOMAS SHERATON.

CABINET-MAKER.

Recommended by many Workmen of the First Abilities in London who have themselves inspected the Work.

THE THIRD EDITION REVISED,

And the whole Embellished with 122 Elegant Copper-Plates.

LONDON:

PRINTED BY T. BENSLEY, BOLT COURT, FLEET STREET,
FOR W. BAYNES (SUCCESSOR TO G. TERRY), 54, PATERNOSTER ROW.
SOLD ALSO BY J. ARCHER, DUBLIN, AND ALL OTHER BOOKSELLERS.

1802

To

CABINET-MAKERS AND UPHOLSTERERS IN GENERAL

GENTLEMEN,

I presume that to publish a Drawing-book answerable to the preceding title page will not require many words to convince you either of the necessity or propriety of the attempt.

Nor will it be requisite to use an ostentatious preface to recommend it to your notice, or to persuade you of the utility of such an undertaking. Therefore, what I have further to say in this Address shall be to give some account of my plan, and point out to you the difference between this and other books which have been published for the assistance and use of Cabinet-makers and Upholsterers.

Books of various designs in cabinet work, ornamented according to the taste of the times in which they were published, have already appeared. But none of these, as far as I know, profess to give any instructions relative to the art of making perspective drawings, or to treat of such geometrical lines as ought to be known by persons of both professions, especially such of them as have a number of men under their direction. Nor have these books given accurate patterns at large for ornaments to enrich and embellish the various pieces of work which frequently occur in the cabinet branch. Such patterns are also highly necessary to copy from by those who would sufficiently qualify themselves for giving a good sketch, or regular drawing, of anything they meet with, or are required to draw for others. Nor indeed would this performance answer so well to the title of a Drawing-book without them. I hope, therefore, that in some degree the above defect is supplied in the following work, and that it will be considered as an enhancement to the real value and usefulness of the Cabinet-Maker and Upholsterer's Drawing-Book to be furnished with a variety of such ornaments as shall serve, both for the purpose of the learner, and also to assist the ideas of those who have occasion to adorn their work in this way.

As I have alluded to some books of designs, it may be proper here just to say something of them. I have seen one which seems to have been published before Chippendale's. I infer this from the antique appearance of the furniture, for there is no date to it; but the title informs us that it was composed by a Society of Cabinet-makers in London. It gives no instructions for drawing in any form, but we may venture to say that those who drew the designs wanted a good share of teaching themselves.

Chippendale's book seems to be next in order to this, but the former is without comparison to it, either as to size or real merit. Chippendale's book has, it is true, given us the proportions of the Five Orders, and lines for two or three cases, which is all it pretends to relative to rules for drawing: and, as for the designs themselves, they are now wholly antiquated and laid aside, though possessed of great merit, according to the times in which they were executed. But it may here be remarked to his credit, that although he has not given rules for drawing in[1] perspective himself yet he was sensible of their importance, and use in designing, and therefore he says in his preface: "Without some knowledge of the rules of perspective, the cabinet-maker cannot make the designs of his work intelligible, nor shew, in a little compass, the whole conduct and effect of the piece. These, therefore, referring to architecture also, ought to be carefully studied by every one who would excel in this branch, since they are the very soul and basis of his art."

After Chippendale's work there appeared, in the year sixty-five, a book of designs for chairs only, though it is called "The Cabinet-Maker's real Friend and Companion," as well as the Chairmaker's. This publication professes to shew their method of striking out all kinds of bevel-work, by which, as the author says, the most ignorant person will be immediately acquainted with what many artists have served seven years to know. But this assertion both exceeds the bounds of modesty and truth, since there is nothing in his directions for bevel-work, which he parades so much about, but what an apprentice boy may be taught by seven hours' proper instructions. With respect to the geometrical view of the Five Orders which he has given, these are useful, and the only thing in his book which at this day is worthy notice; as all his chairs are nearly as old as Chippendale's, and seem to be copied from them.

The succeeding publication to this seems to be Ince's and Mayhew's Book of Designs in Cabinet and Chair Work, with three plates, containing some examples of foliage ornaments, intended for the young designer to copy from, but which can be of no service to any learner now, as they are

[1] This is strictly true of the third edition of Chippendale's book; but the first edition of it, printed in 1754, has given two chairs, a dressing-table, and a book-case in perspective, shewing the lines for drawing them. But why these examples were not continued in the succeeding editions I know not. In the last edition of any work, we naturally expect to see it in its best state, having received its last revisal from the author, or some other hand equal to the task; and therefore it can never be thought unfair for a reader to form his judgment of a book from the last impression. I hope, therefore, this will sufficiently apologise for the above observation.

such kind of ornaments as are wholly laid aside in the cabinet branch, according to the present taste.

The designs in cabinets and chairs are, of course, of the same cast, and therefore have suffered the same fate. Yet, in justice to the work, it may be said to have been a book of merit in its day, though much inferior to Chippendale's, which was a real original, as well as more extensive and masterly in its designs.

In looking over Ince's book I observed two card-tables with some perspective lines, shewing the manner of designing them. These, so far as they go, are a useful attempt ; but certain it is to me, from some experience in teaching, that no person can have the smallest acquaintance with the principles of perspective, merely from seeing two or three lines joined to a plate, without proper instructions by letter-press. It is true, a description is given of these lines in the 7th page of his book, but not equal to what is absolutely requisite to such as have no previous acquaintance with the art ; and those that have, will not require that which can give them no assistance. Properly speaking then, what is done in this book, relative to perspective lines, can only serve as a hint to the workman, that this art is essential in designing.

In the year 1788 was published, "The Cabinet-maker's and Upholsterer's Guide," in which are found no directions for drawing in any form, nor any pretensions to it. The whole merit of the performance rests on the designs, with a short description to each plate prefixed. Some of these designs are not without merit, though it is evident that the perspective is, in some instances, erroneous. But, notwithstanding the late date of Hepplewhite's book, if we compare some of the designs, particularly the chairs, with the newest taste, we shall find that this work has already caught the decline, and, perhaps, in a little time will suddenly die in the disorder. This instance may serve to convince us of that fate which all books of the same kind will ever be subject to. Yet it must be owned, that books of this sort have their usefulness for a time ; and, when through change of fashions they are become obsolete, they serve to shew the taste of former ages.

I shall now conclude this account of books of designs with observing, that in the same year was given a quarto book of different pieces of furniture, with the Cabinet-maker's London Book of Prices ; and, considering that it did not make its appearance under the title of a Book of Designs, but only to illustrate the prices, it certainly lays claim to merit, and does honour to the publishers.

Upon the whole then, if the intended publication, which now petitions your patronage and support, be so compiled and composed as fully to answer, and also to merit, the title which has been given to it, I think it will be found greatly to supply the defects of those books now mentioned, and will appear to be on as lasting a foundation as can well be expected in a work of this kind. For instance, the first part, which provides the workman with geometrical lines, applied to various purposes in the cabinet branch, cannot be subject to alteration any more than the principles of reason itself. The same may be said of Perspective; the subject of the second part. This art, being founded on Geometry and Optics, may be improved in its practice but its fundamental principles can never be altered, any more than the nature of vision itself.

As to the designs in furniture contained in part third, these are indeed liable to change; nor is it in the power of any man to provide against it, by making such drawings as will always be thought new. Yet the instructions given on the manufacturing part being founded on real experience and practice, will be much the same at all times. It also adds to the usefulness of the designs, that I have in general given their geometrical dimensions, either laid down on the ground, or other scale lines adapted for that purpose, or else described in the letterpress. So that no person, however ignorant of perspective, can easily mistake the perspective for the geometrical measurements, or be at any loss to know the general sizes of such pieces as shall be introduced.

In proceeding however, with the first edition, I found that to give scales for the perspective heights and widths could not be done, in many instances, without encumbering the designs in such a way as greatly to hurt their appearance. To remove this inconvenience, and to assist those who have a little knowledge of perspective, in obtaining the true measurements of such designs or engravings as may have no scales to them, I have shewn, in the perspective part, that this may be easily done, by finding the vanishing points and distance, and tracing their visuals forward to the ground line. In the first edition this is done at the end of the Appendix, because its usefulness did not strike me till I came to that part of the work.

With respect to mouldings and various ornaments, the subject of the fourth part, it is granted that these are of a changeable kind. Yet it is pretty evident that materials for proper ornaments are now brought to such perfection as will not, in future, admit of much, if any, degree of improvement, though they may, by the skill and touch of the ingenious hand, be varied, ad infinitum, to suit any taste at any time.

Lastly, I would entreat leave gratefully to acknowledge the general encouragement I have been favoured with in going through the first edition: and though my vast expense has deprived me of the emolument that might have been expected for so numerous a subscription, yet it is some consolation to be conscious that I have spared no expense, nor withheld anything in my power to do the work justice, and give satisfaction to the public.

And I have the additional happiness to know, from several testimonies, the full approbation that the work has obtained in the judgment of the candid and skilful. And, notwithstanding the ill nature of some, who hate to speak well of anything but their own productions, I only wish that a comparison be made with any other book hitherto published for the use of Cabinet-makers and Upholsterers, and then it will sufficiently speak for itself.

And now, in going through this third edition, it is still my steady intention to contribute as much as I can towards improving the work, and rendering it as complete as is in the power of,

Gentlemen,

Your humble Servant,

THOMAS SHERATON.

CONTENTS

SHERATON

THE CABINET-MAKER AND UPHOLSTERER'S DRAWING-BOOK

CONTENTS

DESIGNS FOR HOUSEHOLD FURNITURE

SHERATON

Drawing-Room Chairs and Sofa

Chaises Longues

SHERATON

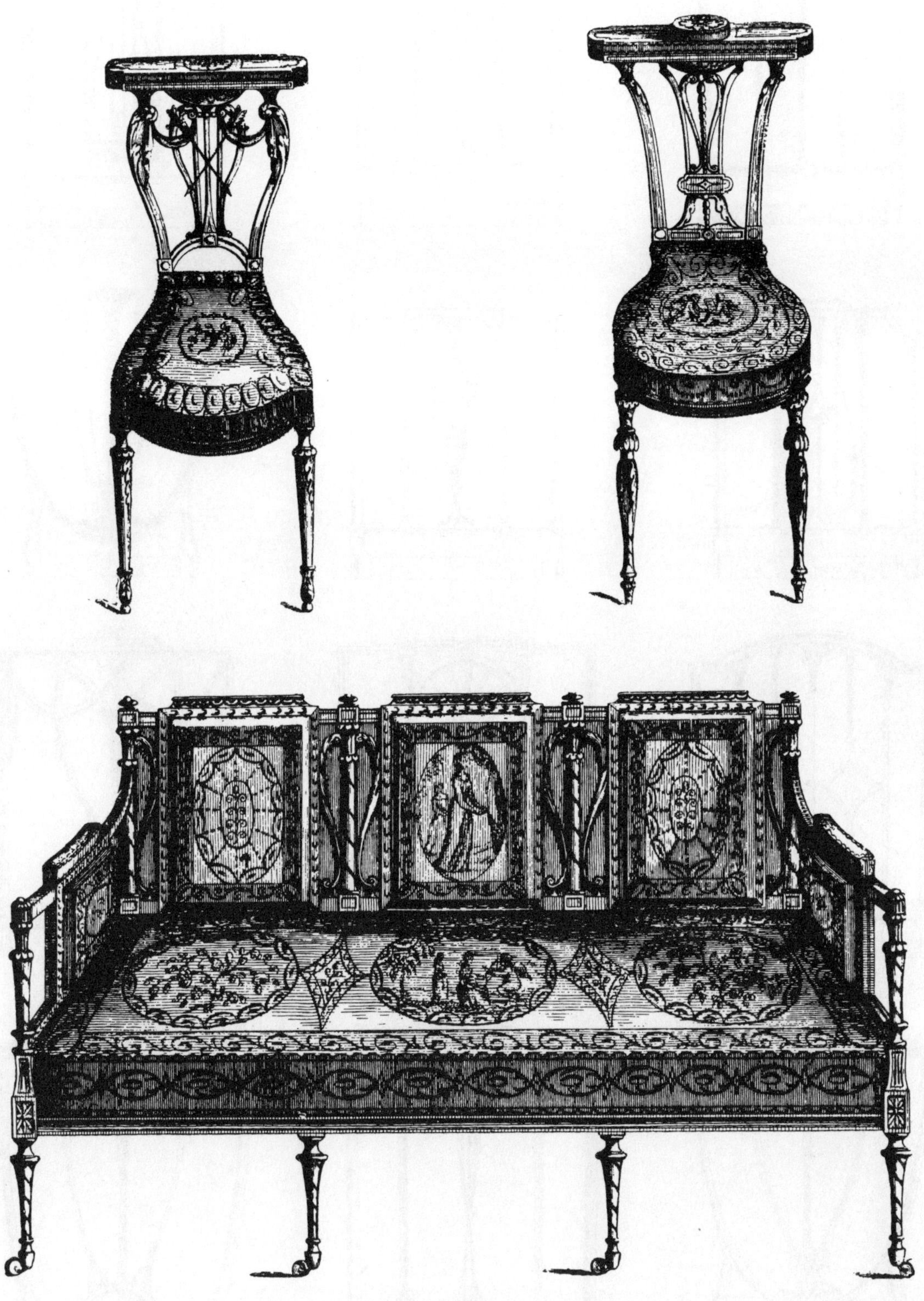

Conversation Chairs and Sofa

SHERATON

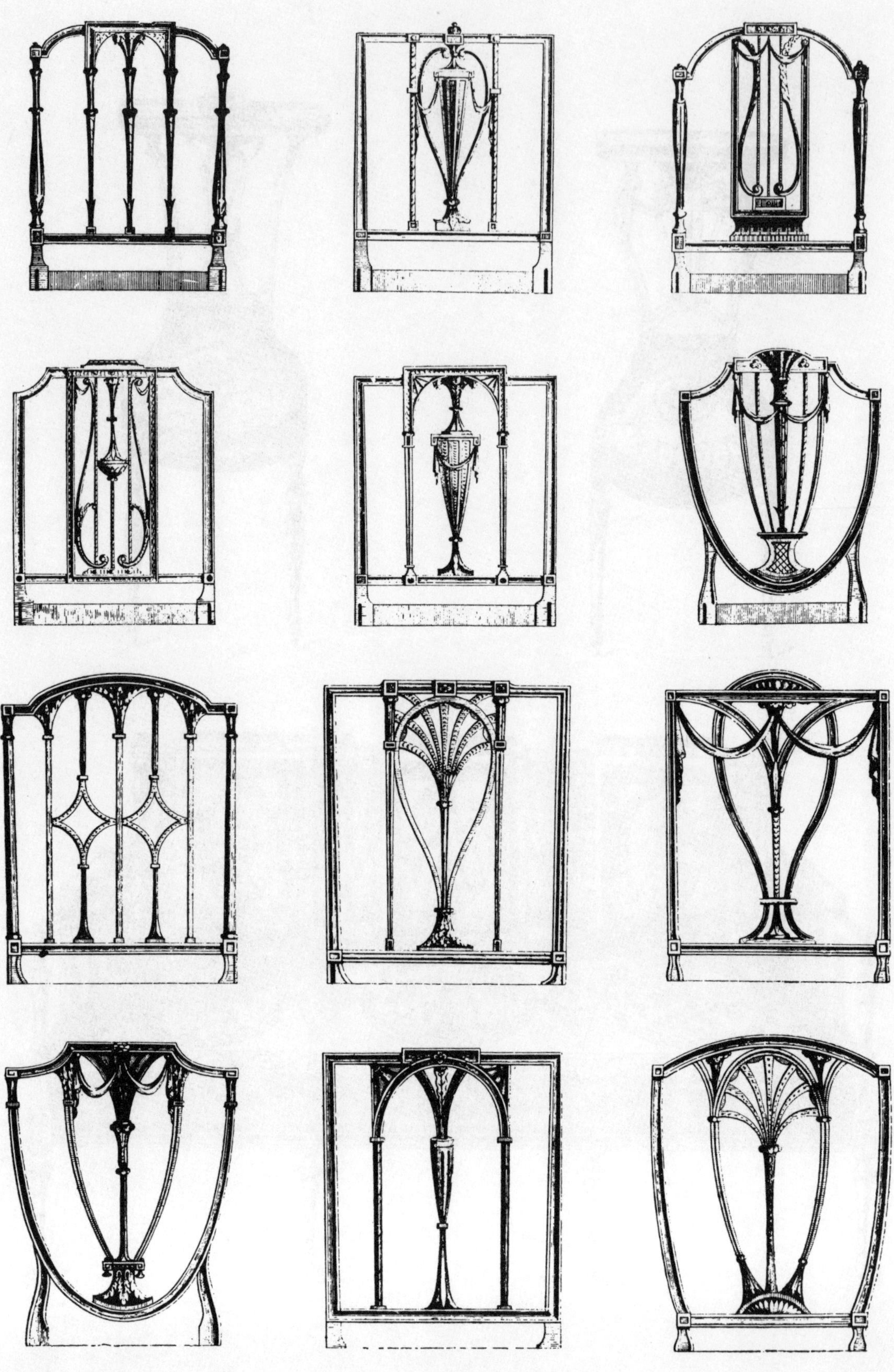

Backs for Parlour Chairs

SHERATON

Backs for Painted Chairs

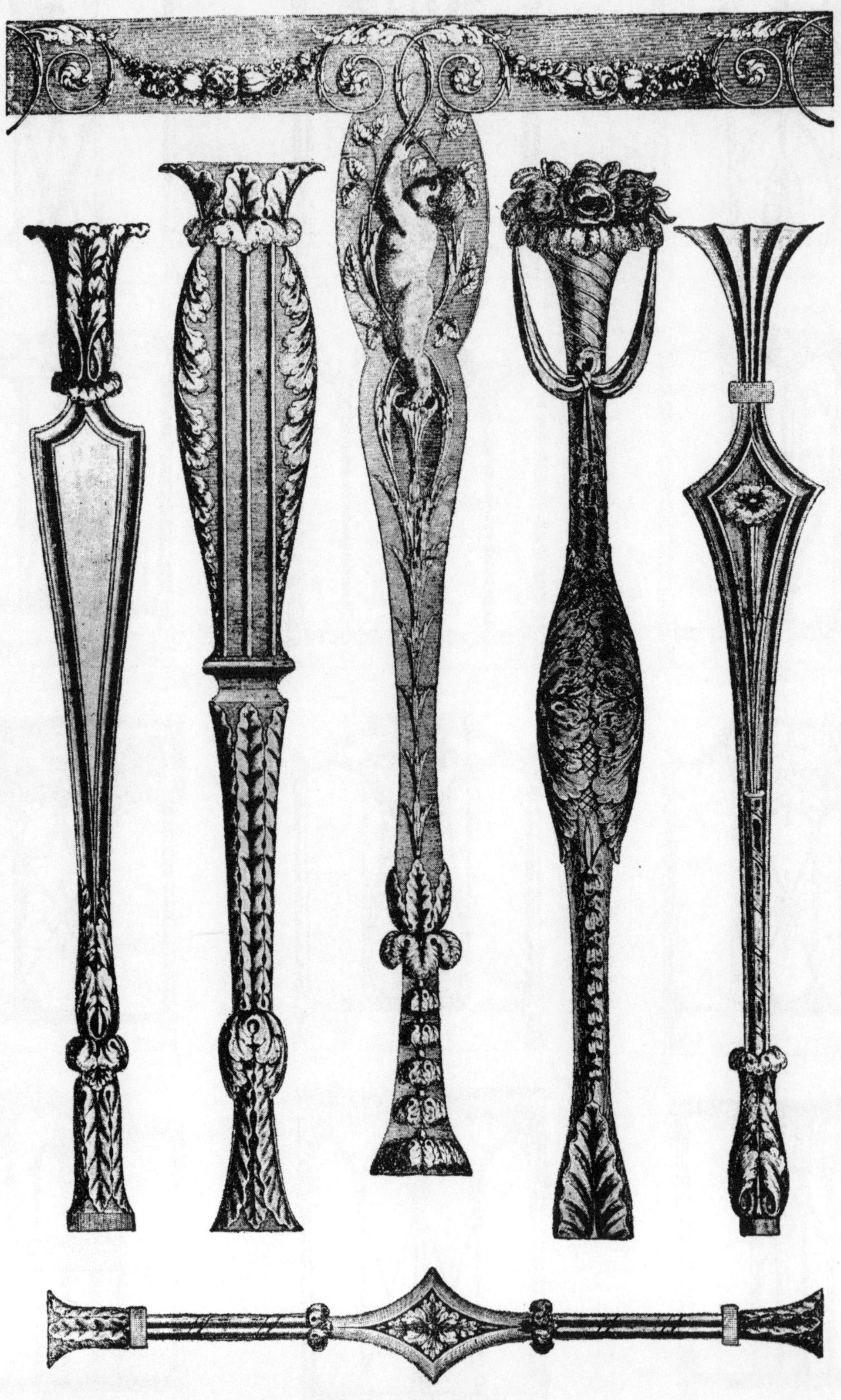

Splads for Painted and Mahogany Chairs

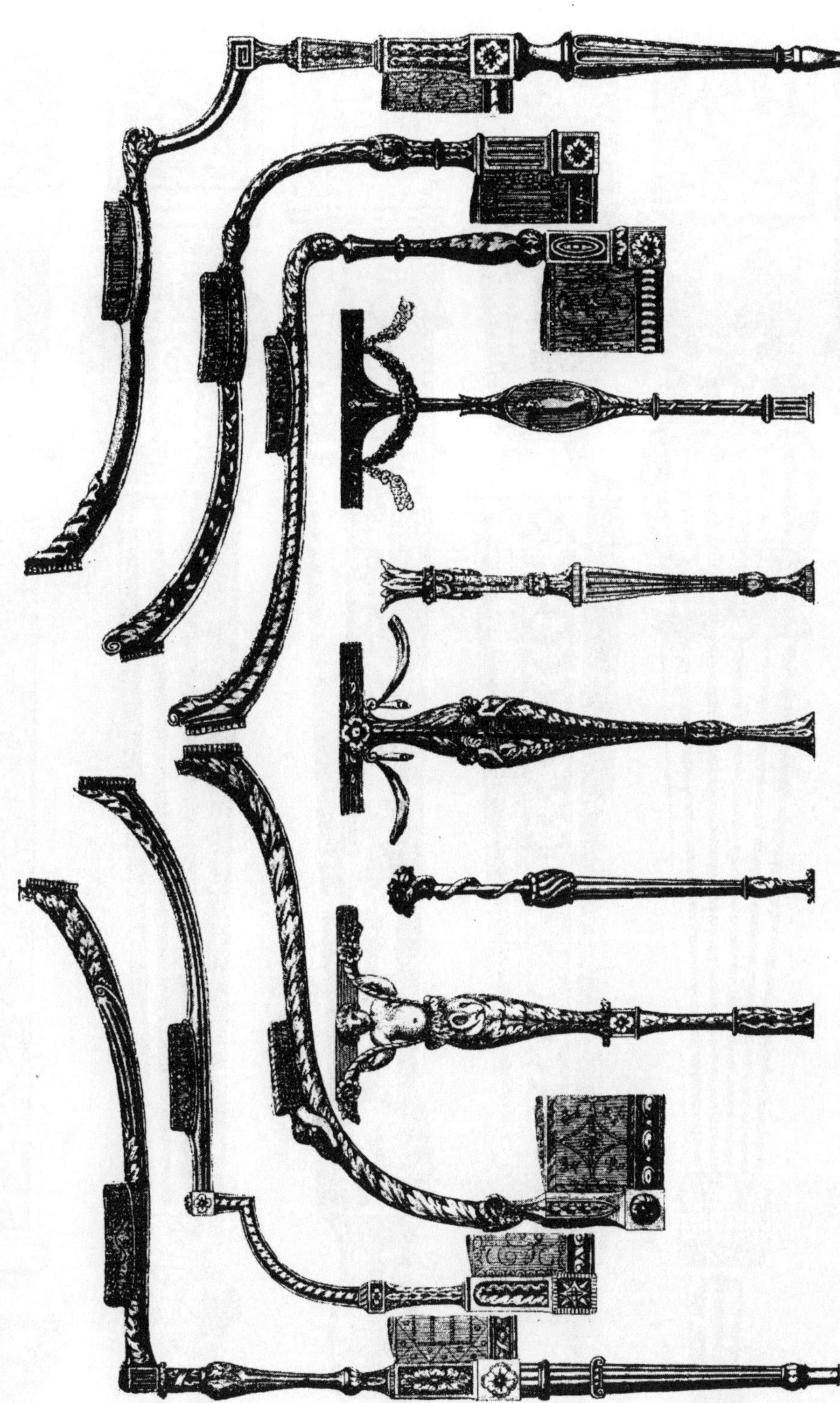

Stumps and Elbows for Drawing-Room Chairs

Chair Legs

SHERATON

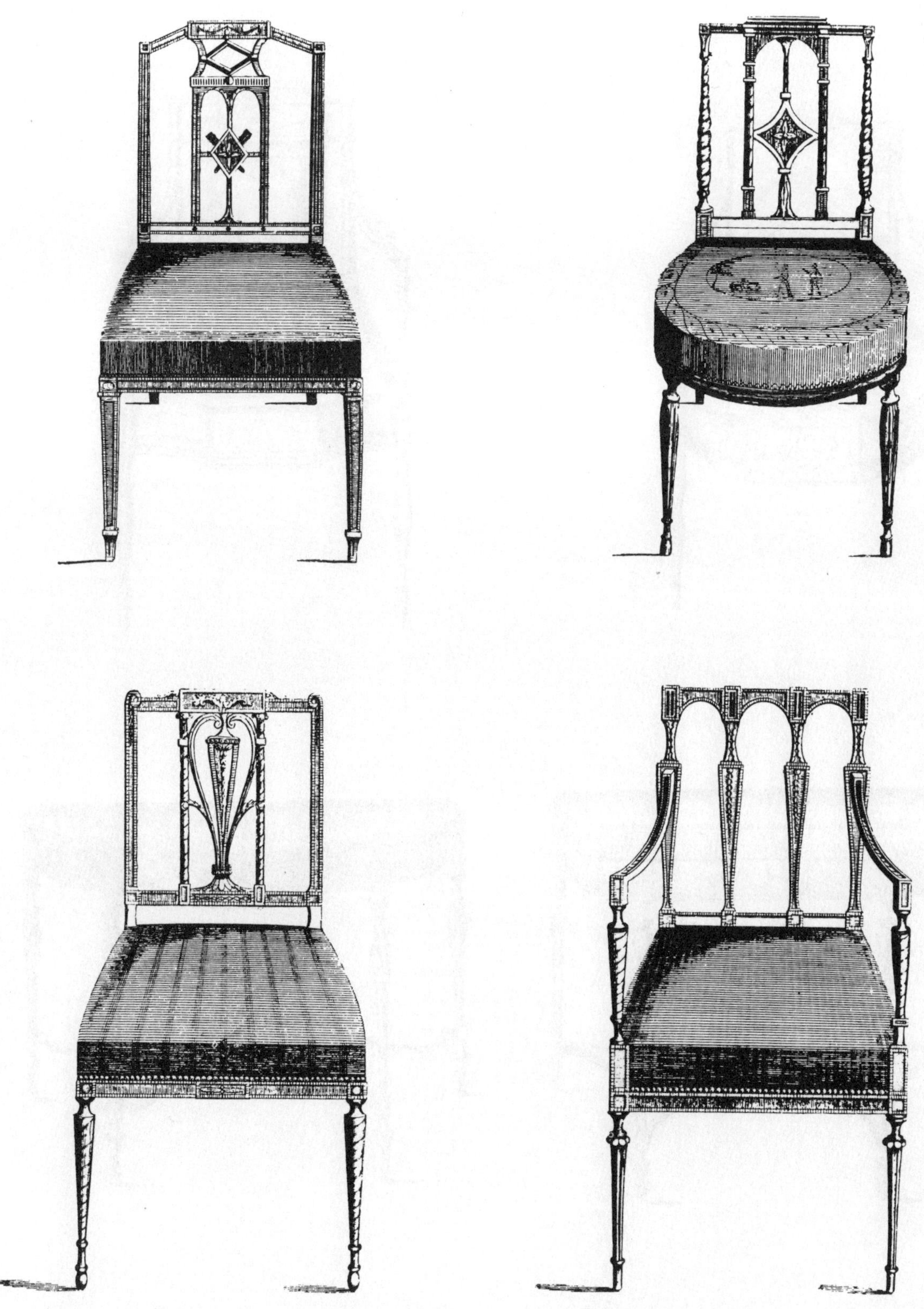

Three Parlour Chairs and a Drawing-room Chair

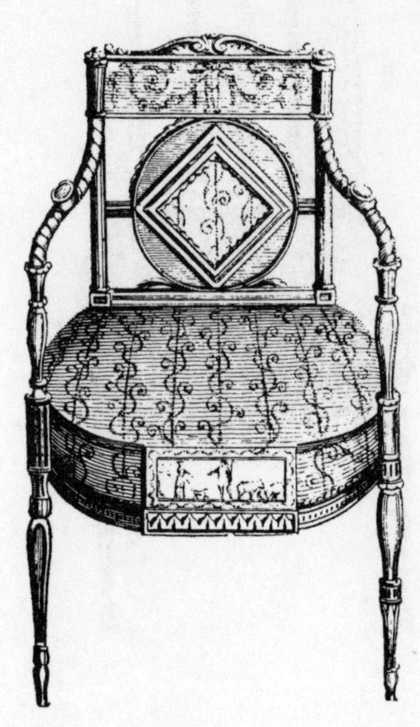

Drawing-room Chairs and Pier Tables

SHERATON

A Drawing Table, a Cabinet, and Tripod Candlestands

SHERATON

A Commode Dressing Table, a Chamber-horse, a Lady's Dressing Writing Table, a Writing Table, and a Cylinder Desk and Bookcase

SHERATON

Card Tables, Lady's Cabinet, showing inside fittings, and a Kidney Table

Ornament for a Table, Secretary and Bookcase, and Clock Cases

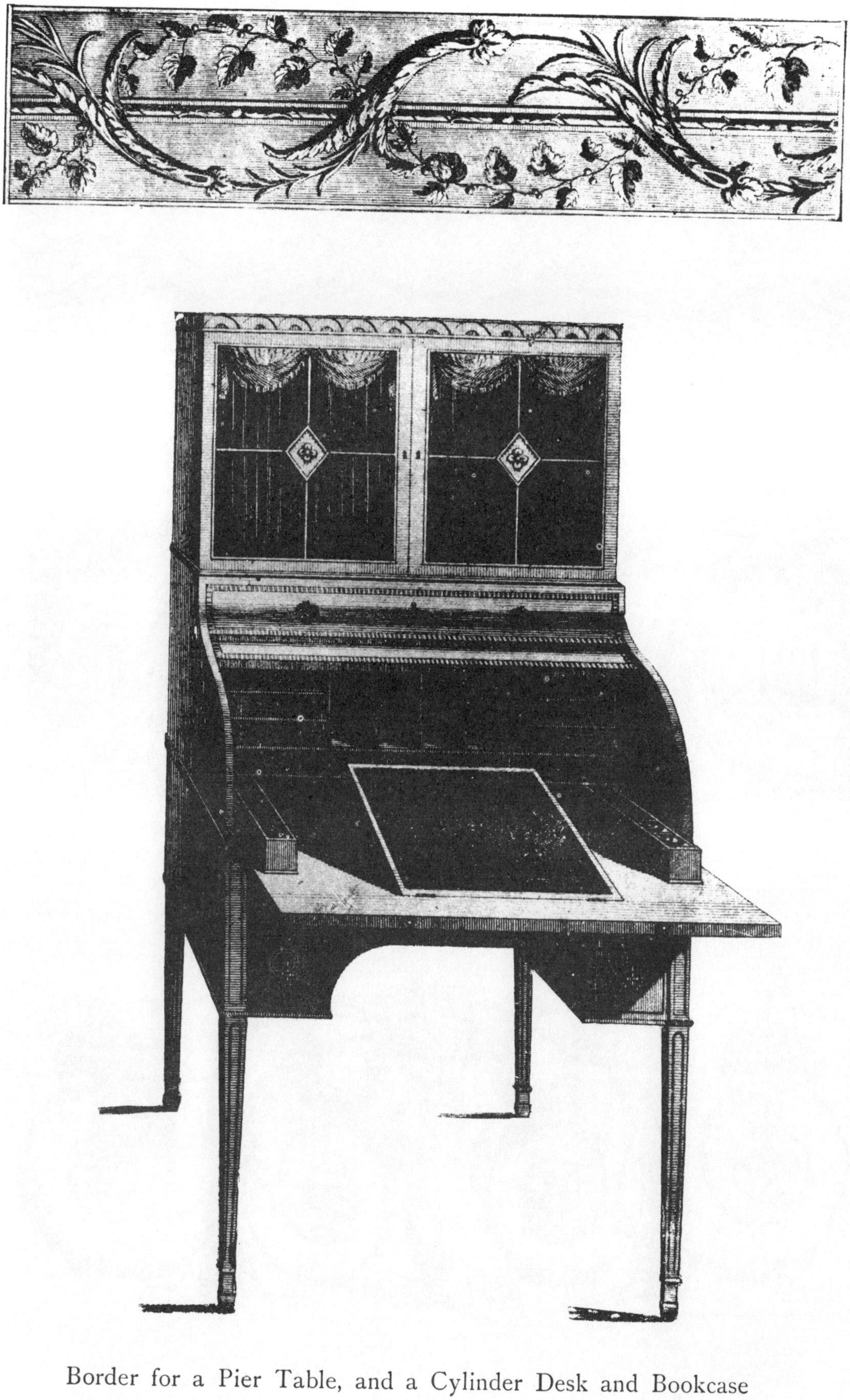

Border for a Pier Table, and a Cylinder Desk and Bookcase

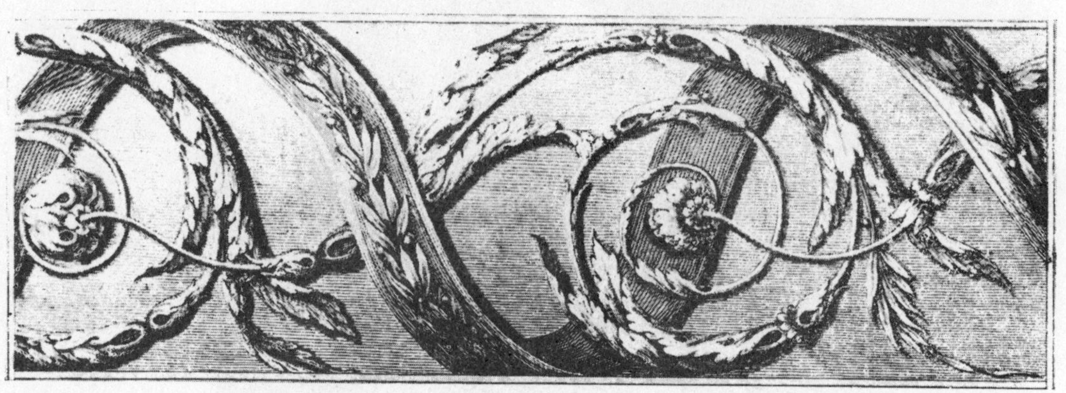

Borders for Pier Tables

SHERATON

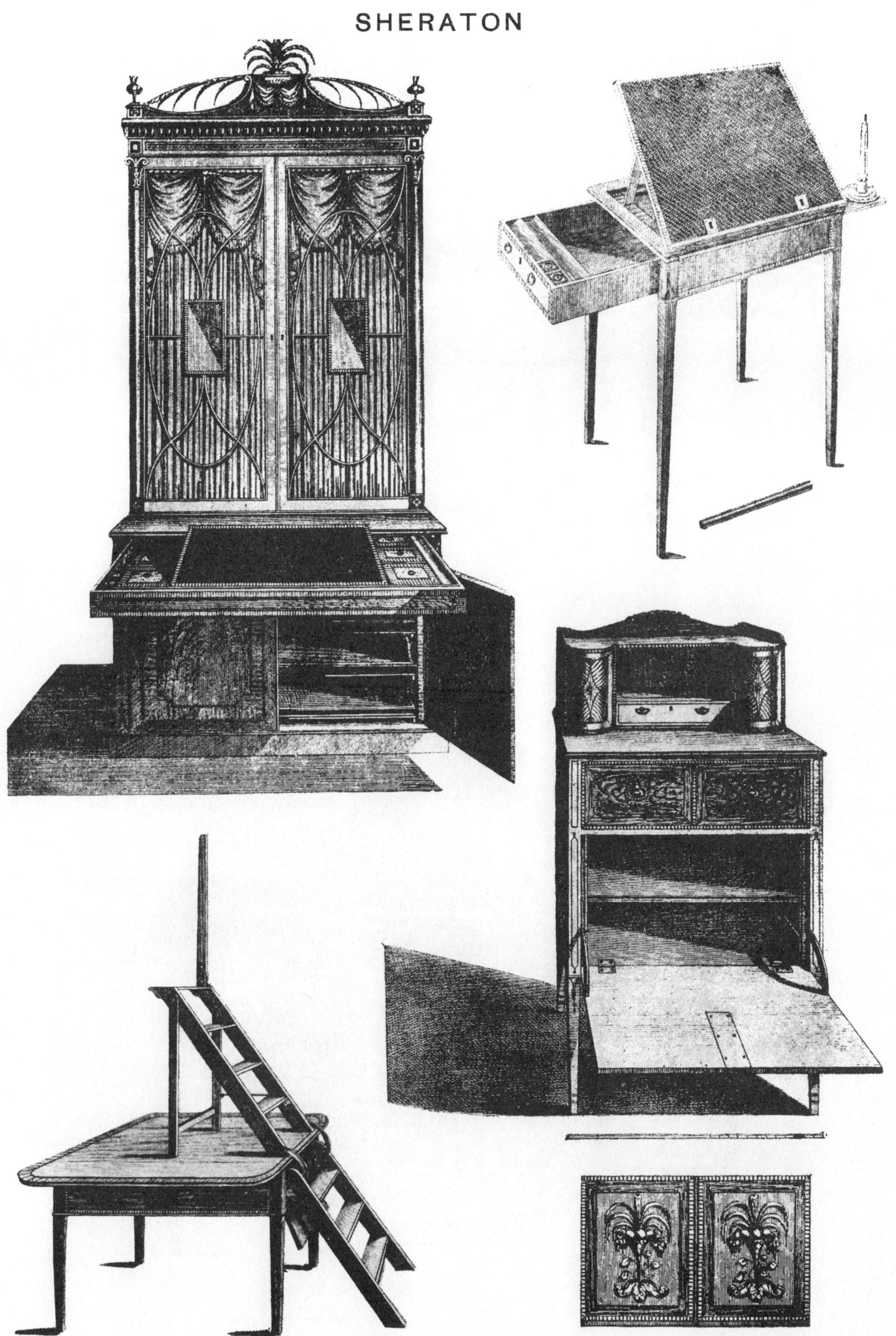

Bookcase and Writing Drawers, Drawing Table, Lady's Secretary with carved front, and Library Steps and Pembroke Table

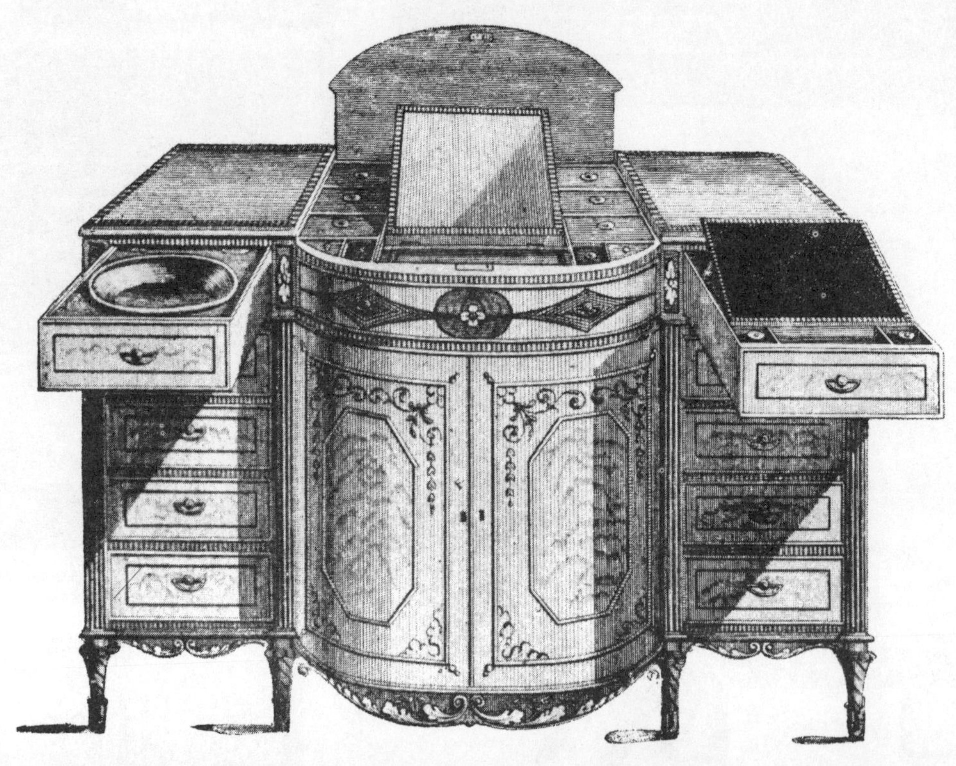

A Library Table and a Lady's Dressing Commode

SHERATON

Horse Fire Screens and a Library Table with Secretary Drawers

SHERATON

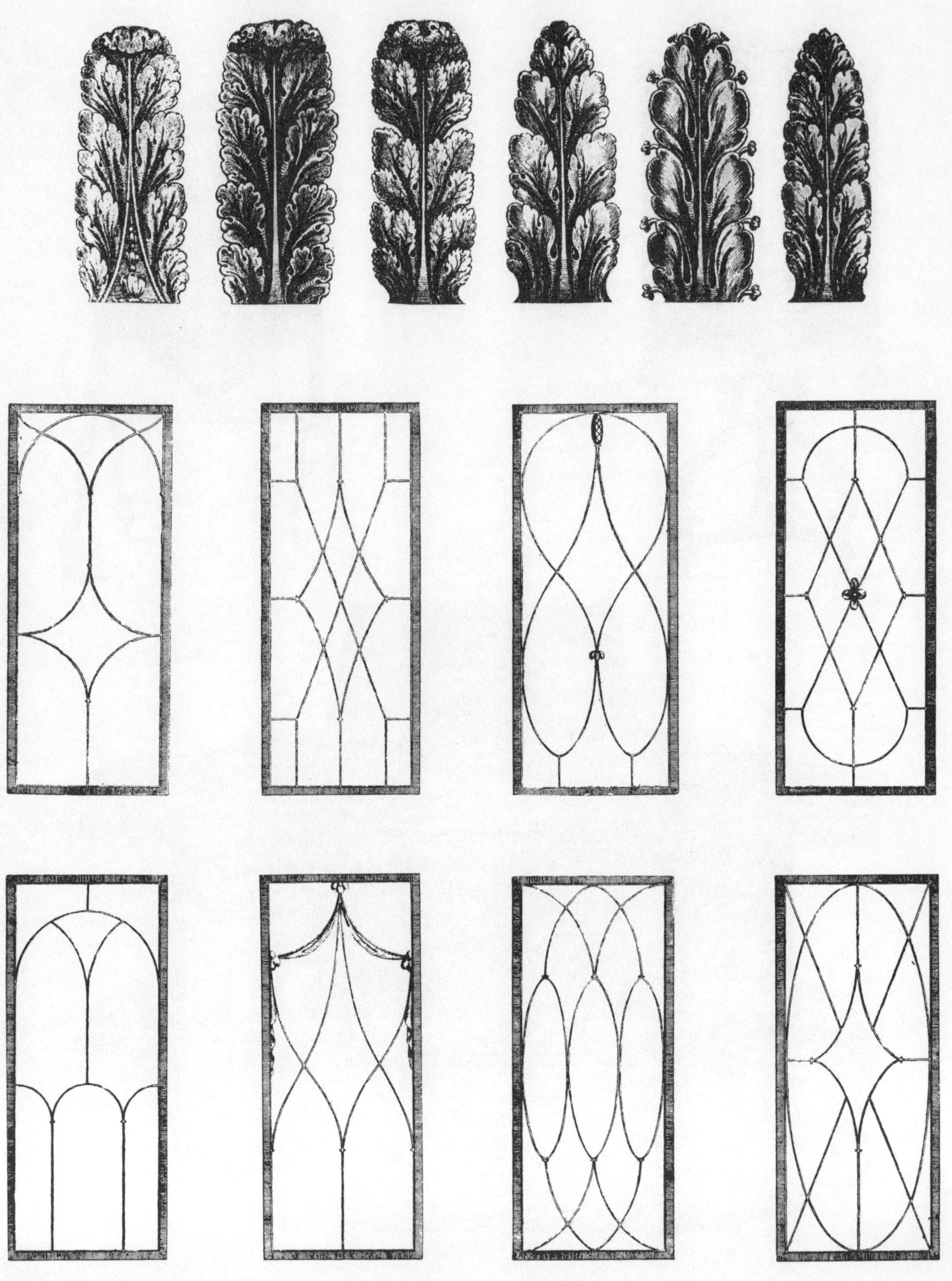

Various Leaves and Bookcase Doors

SHERATON

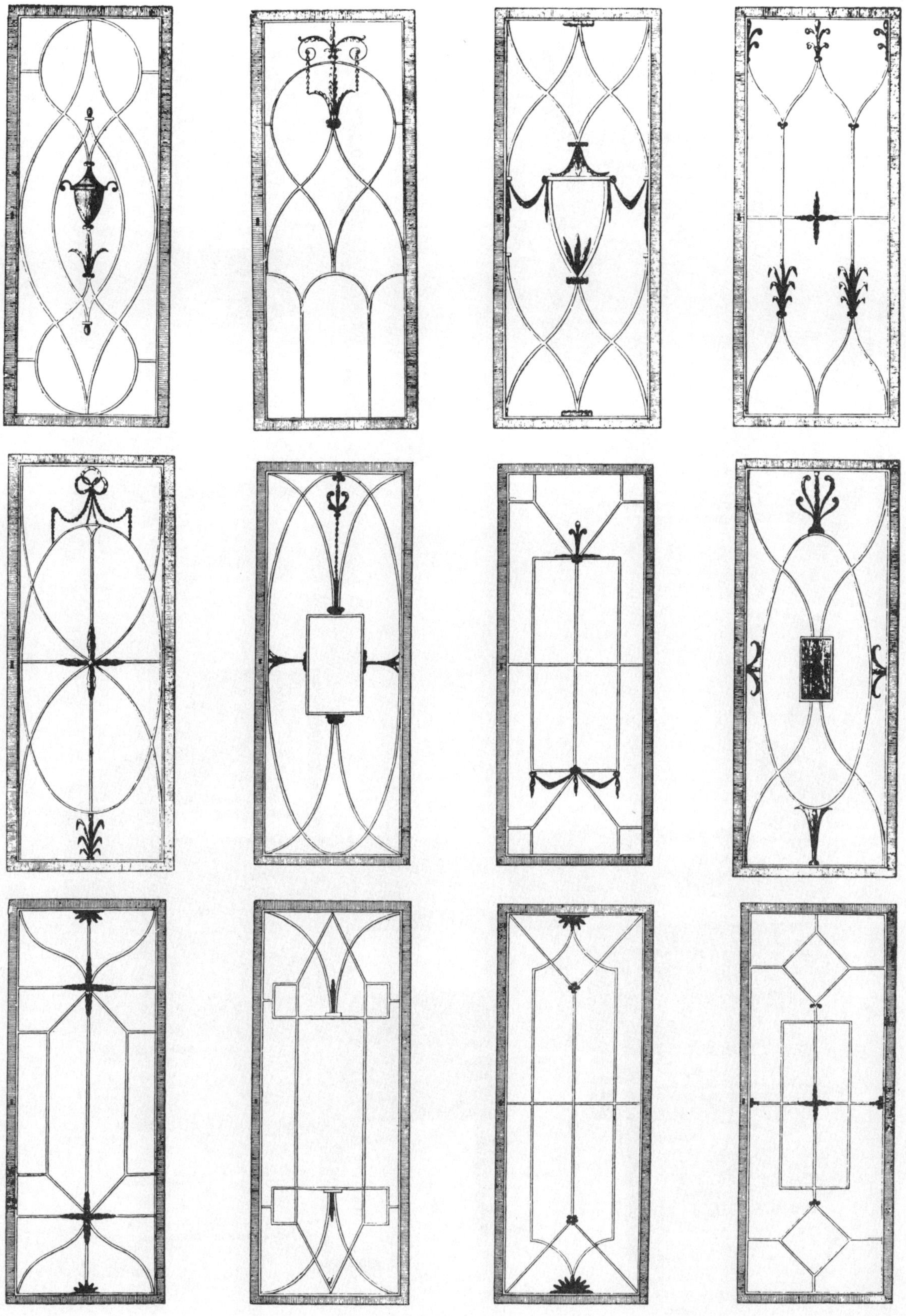

Bookcase Doors

SHERATON

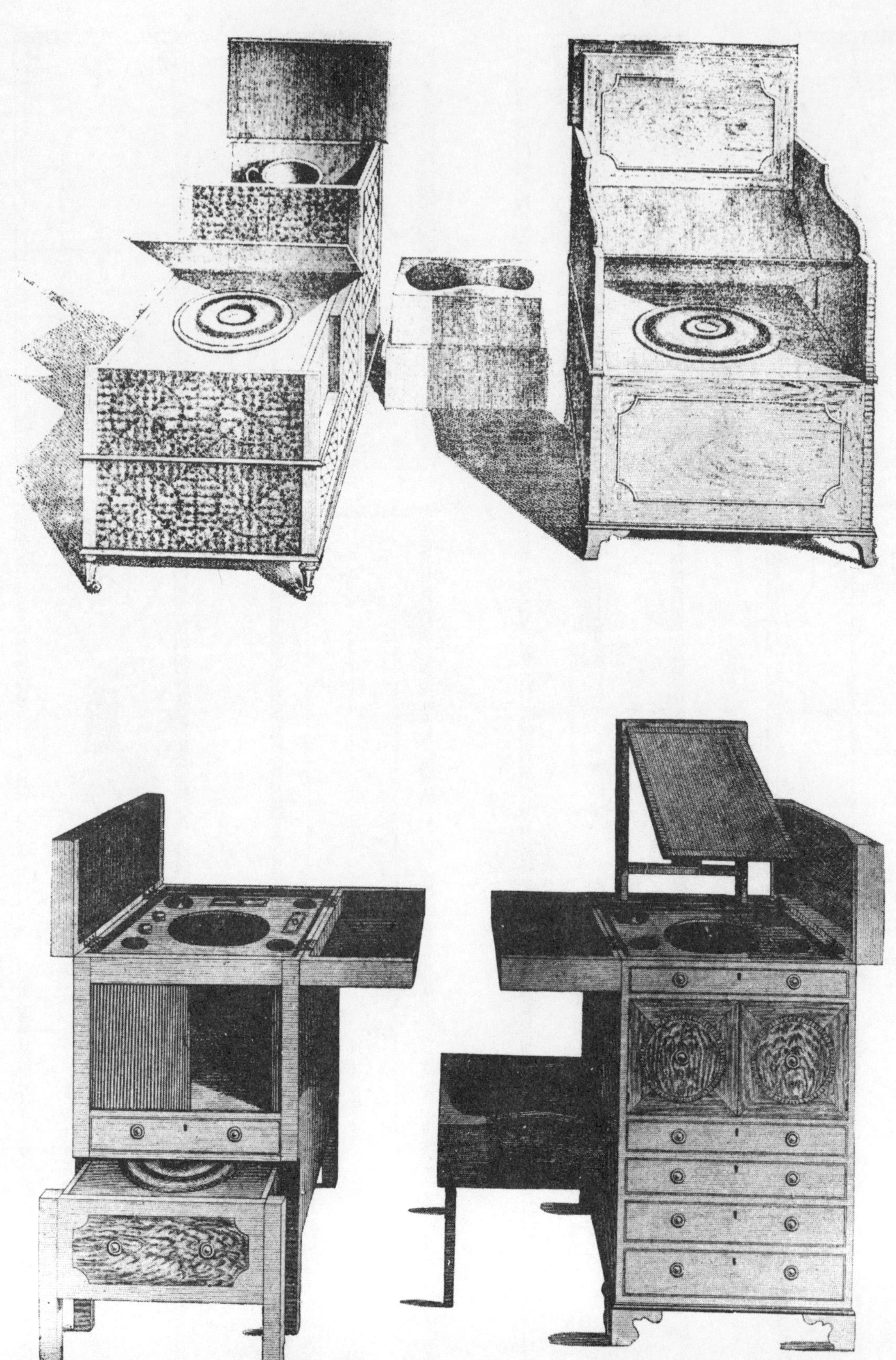

New Bed-steps, a Bidet Dressing Table, and a Night-Table Basin-stand

SHERATON

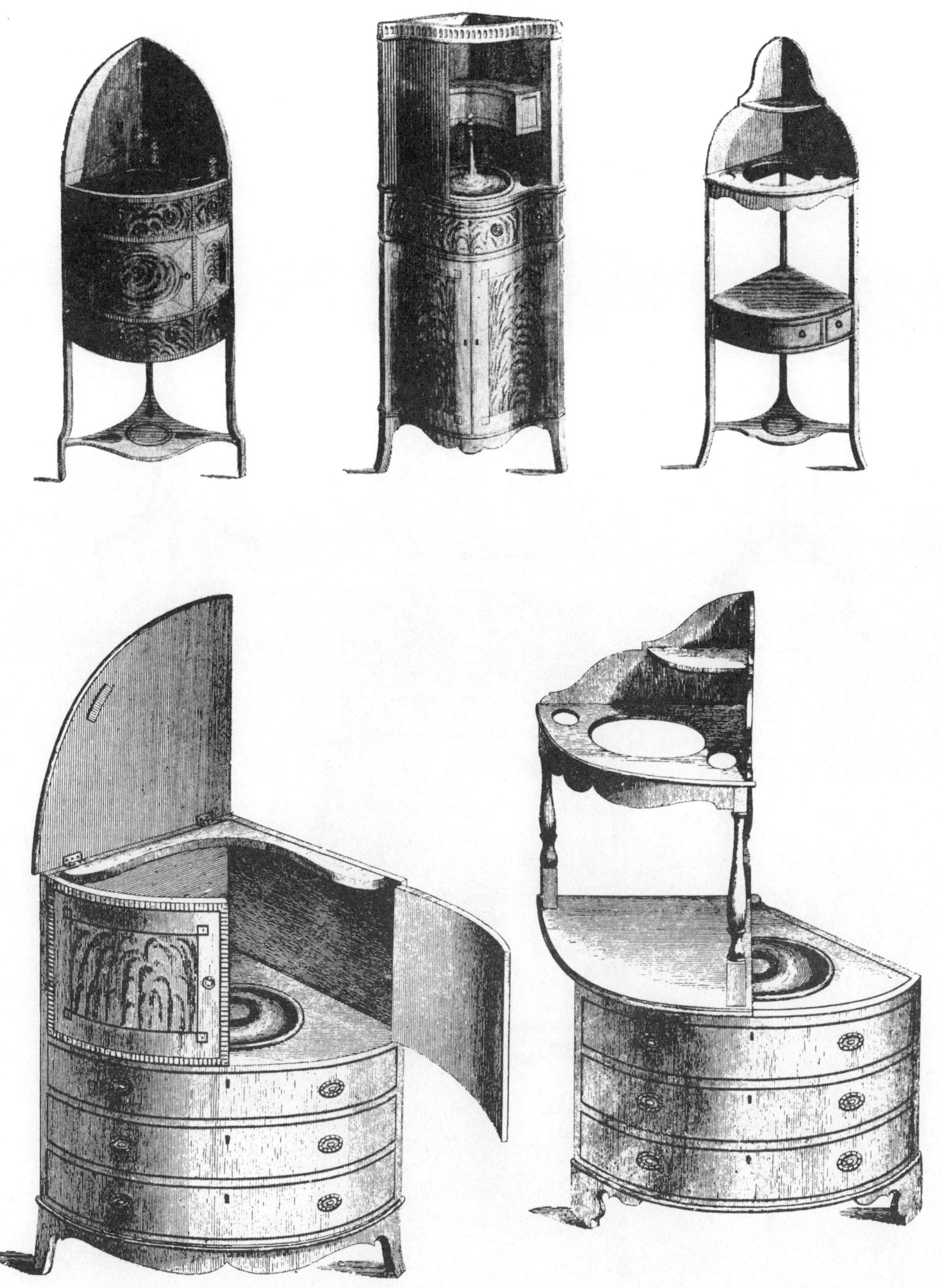

Corner Basin-stands and Corner Night Tables

Tripod Fire Screens and a Cylinder Wash-hand Table

SHERATON

A Gentleman's Secretary and a Library Case

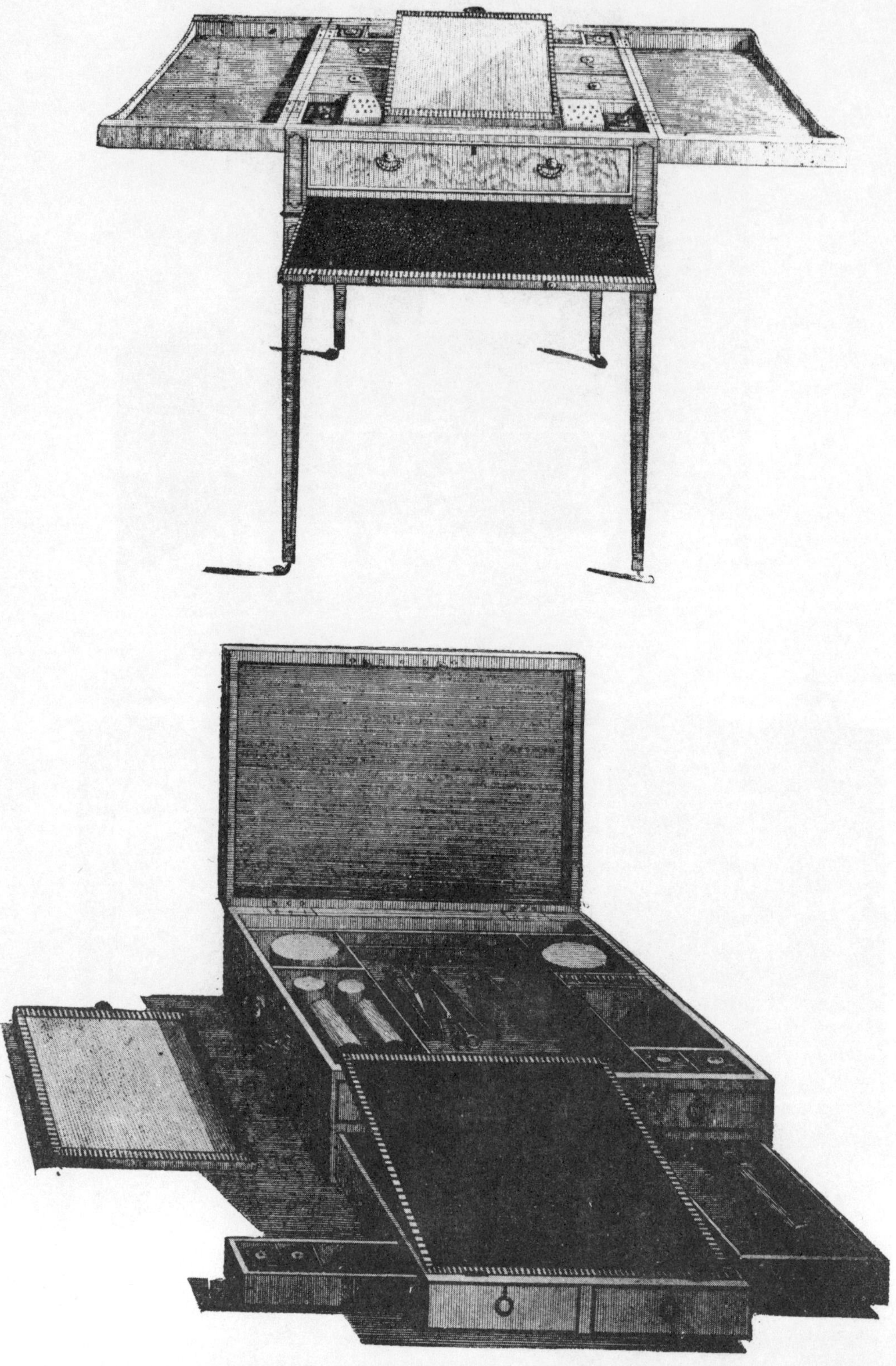

Dressing Table and a Lady's Travelling Box

SHERATON

The Universal Table and a Harlequin Pembroke Table

SHERATON

A Cabinet and a Dressing Chest

SHERATON

A Lady's Combined Dressing Table and a Dressing Chest

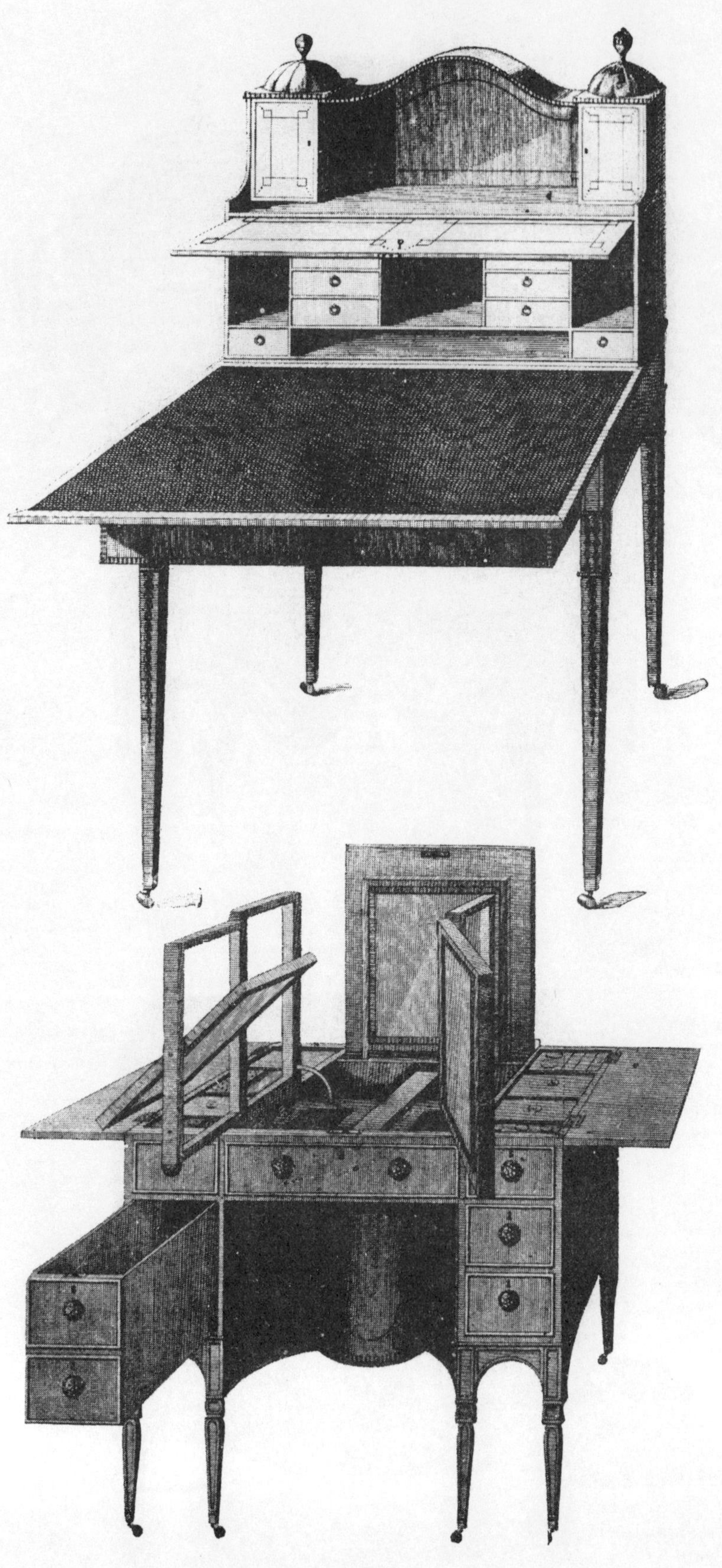

Lady's Cabinet and Writing Table, and Lady's Dressing Table

SHERATON

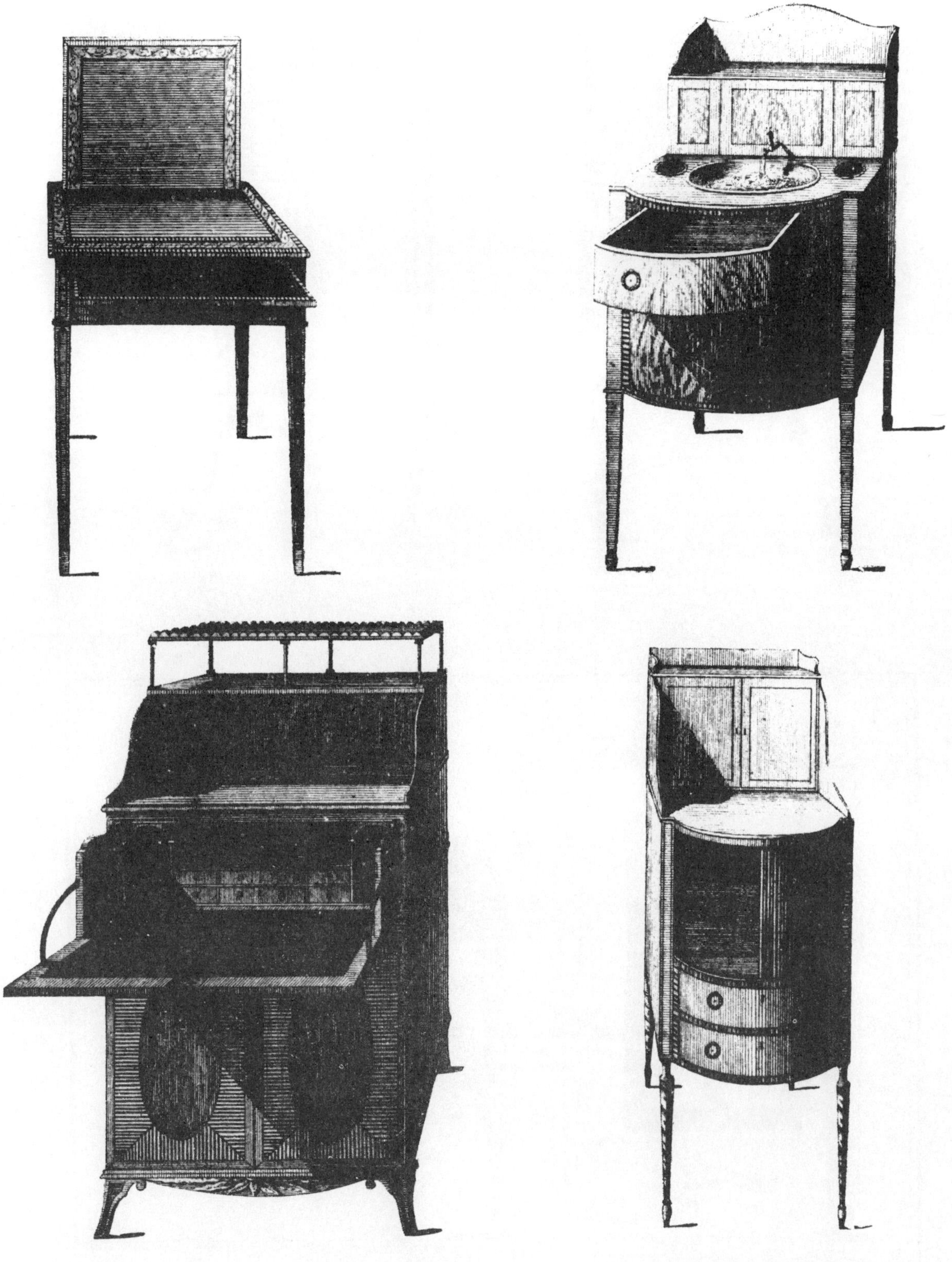

A Screen Table, a Wash Stand, a Lady's Secretary, a Pot Cupboard

SHERATON

Horse Dressing Glass and Writing Table, Horse Dressing Glass, and a Lady's Writing Table

SHERATON

Ladies' Work-Tables and a Pembroke Table

Sideboard, showing Spring for Secret Drawer, and a Sideboard Table

SHERATON

Sideboard with Vase Knife-cases, and Sideboard with Mahogany Vase underneath to hold Bottles

SHERATON

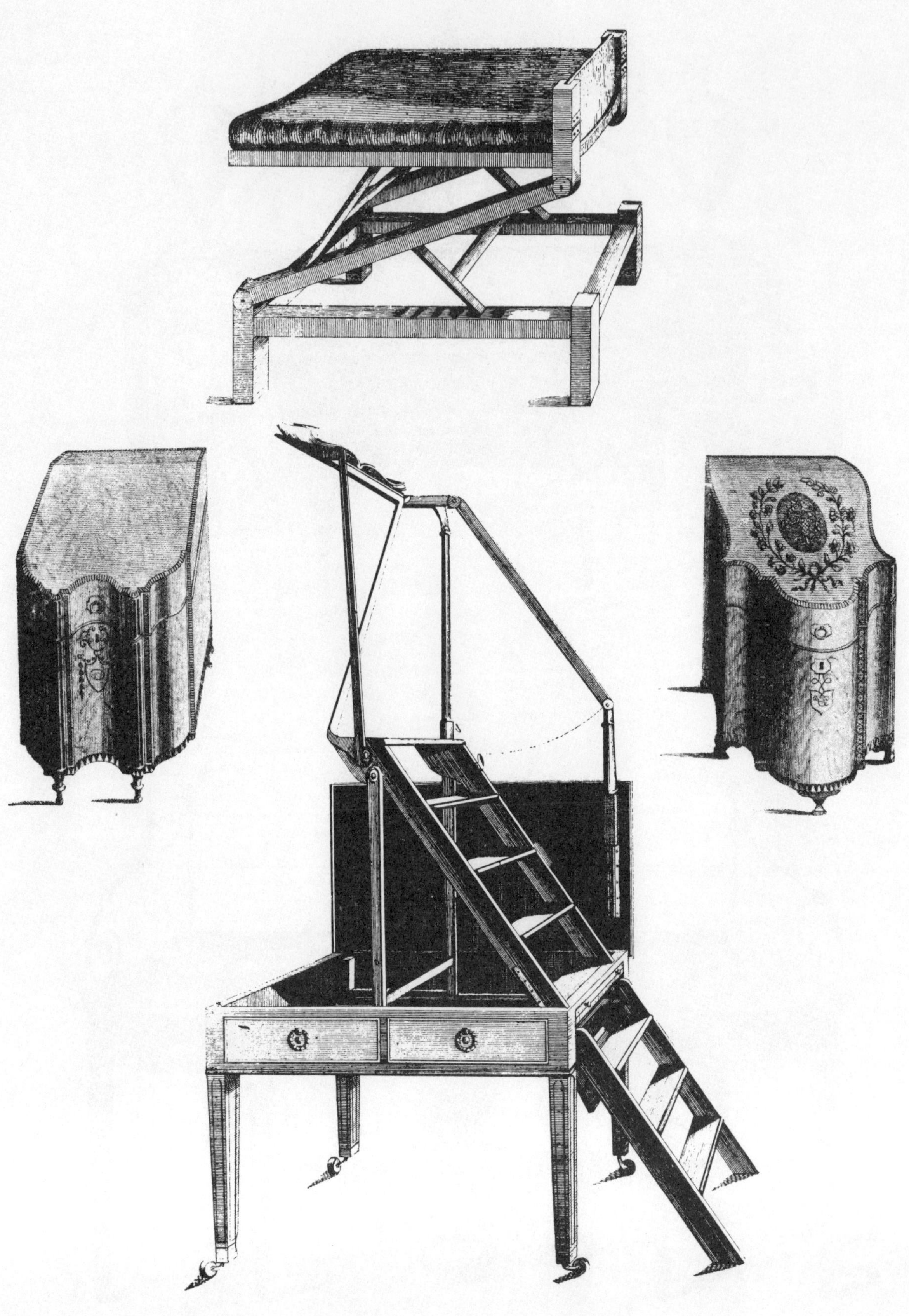

A Gouty Stool, Knife-cases, and Library Steps and Table

SHERATON

A Wardrobe, and Cornices, Curtains, and Drapery for Drawing-Room Windows

The Two Ends of a Drawing-Room

The Two Sides of a Drawing-Room

A View of the Prince of Wales's Chinese Drawing-Room
View of south end of same Room

SHERATON

A Commode

An English State Bed

A Sofa Bed

A French State Bed, obliquely situated to the picture; and an Elliptic Bed for a single Lady

SHERATON

A Design for a Bed

A Duchesse

A Summer Bed in two Compartments

An Alcove Bed

SHERATON

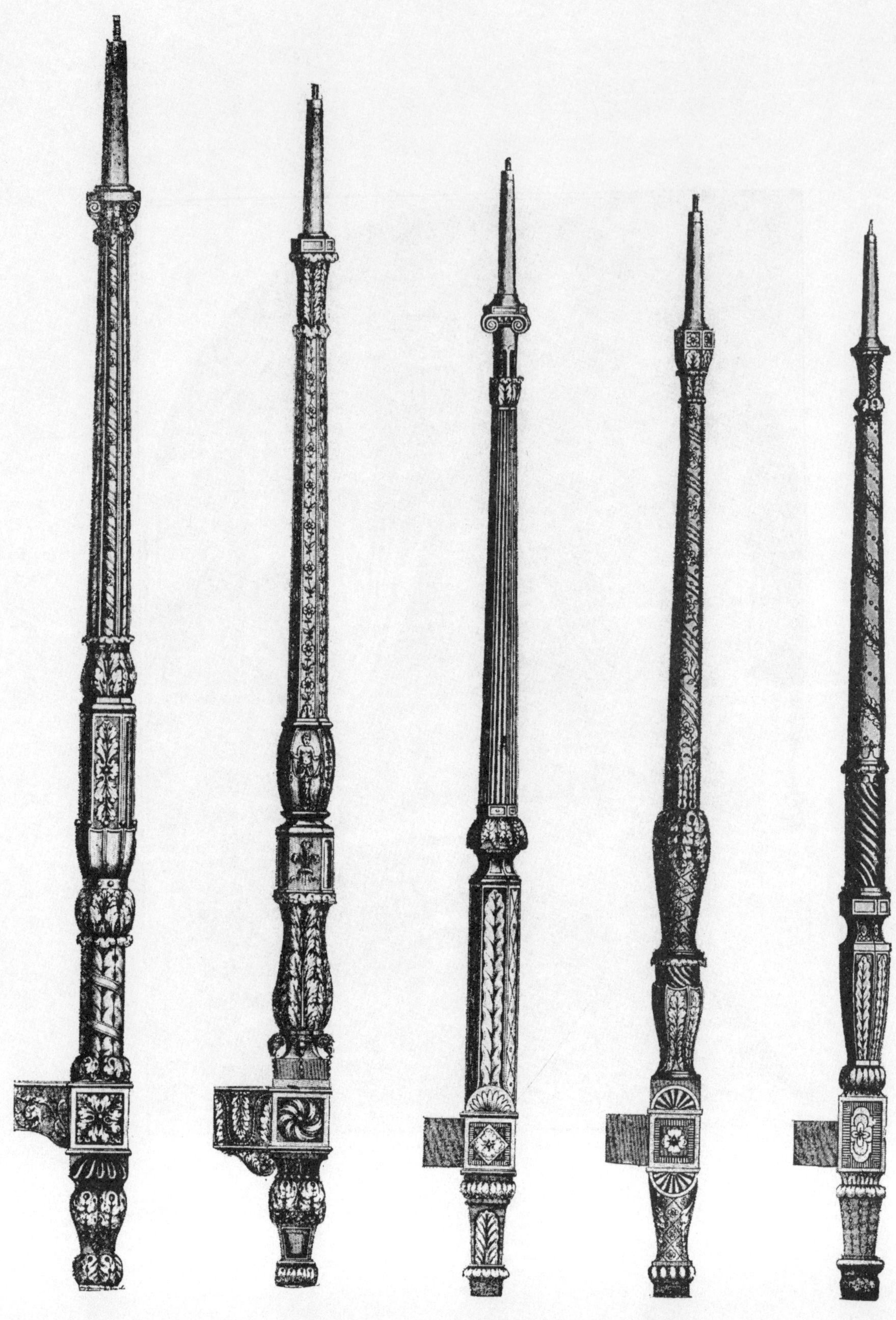

Bed Pillars

SHERATON

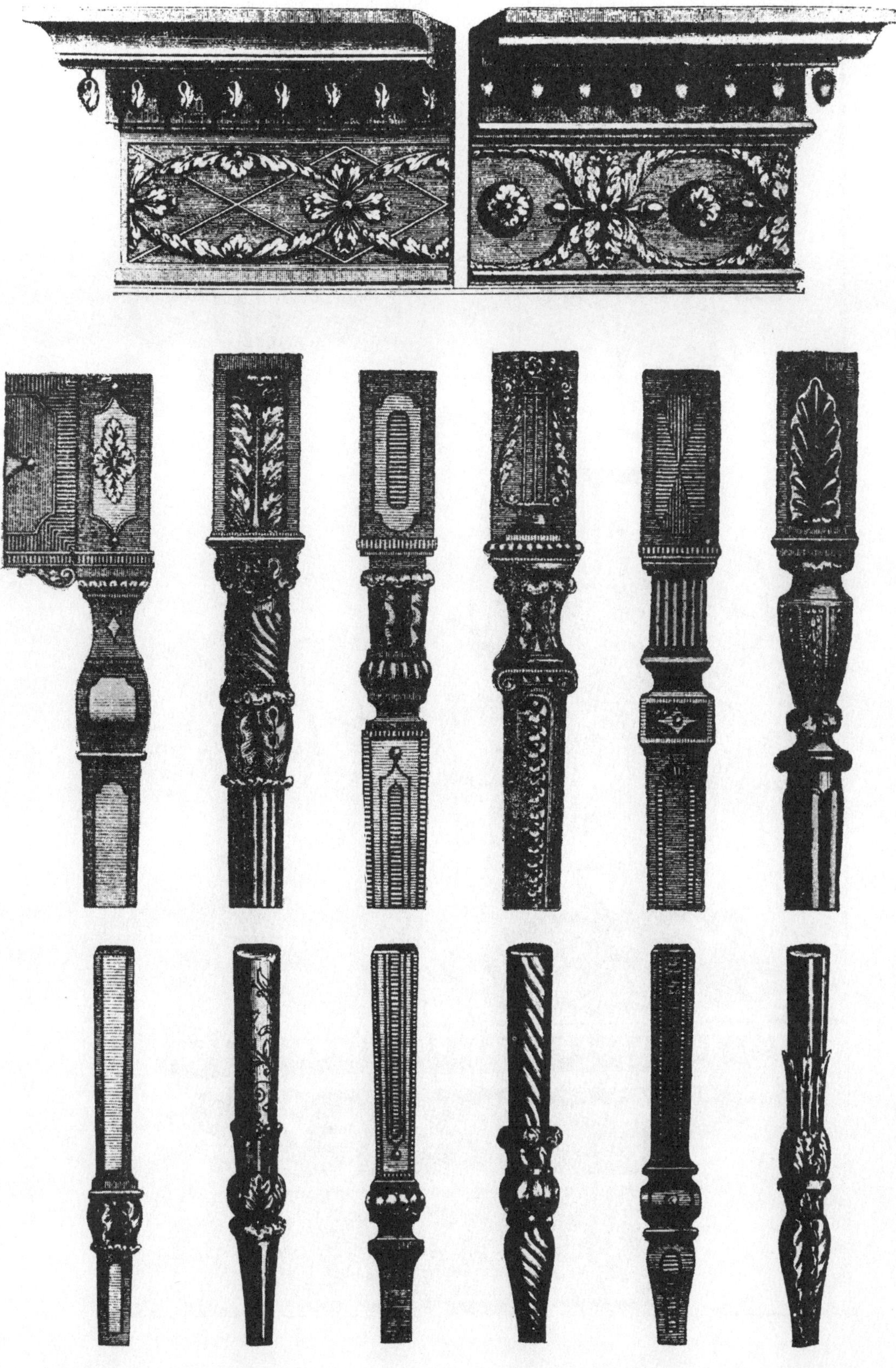

Cornices for Friezes, and Legs for Pier and Card Tables

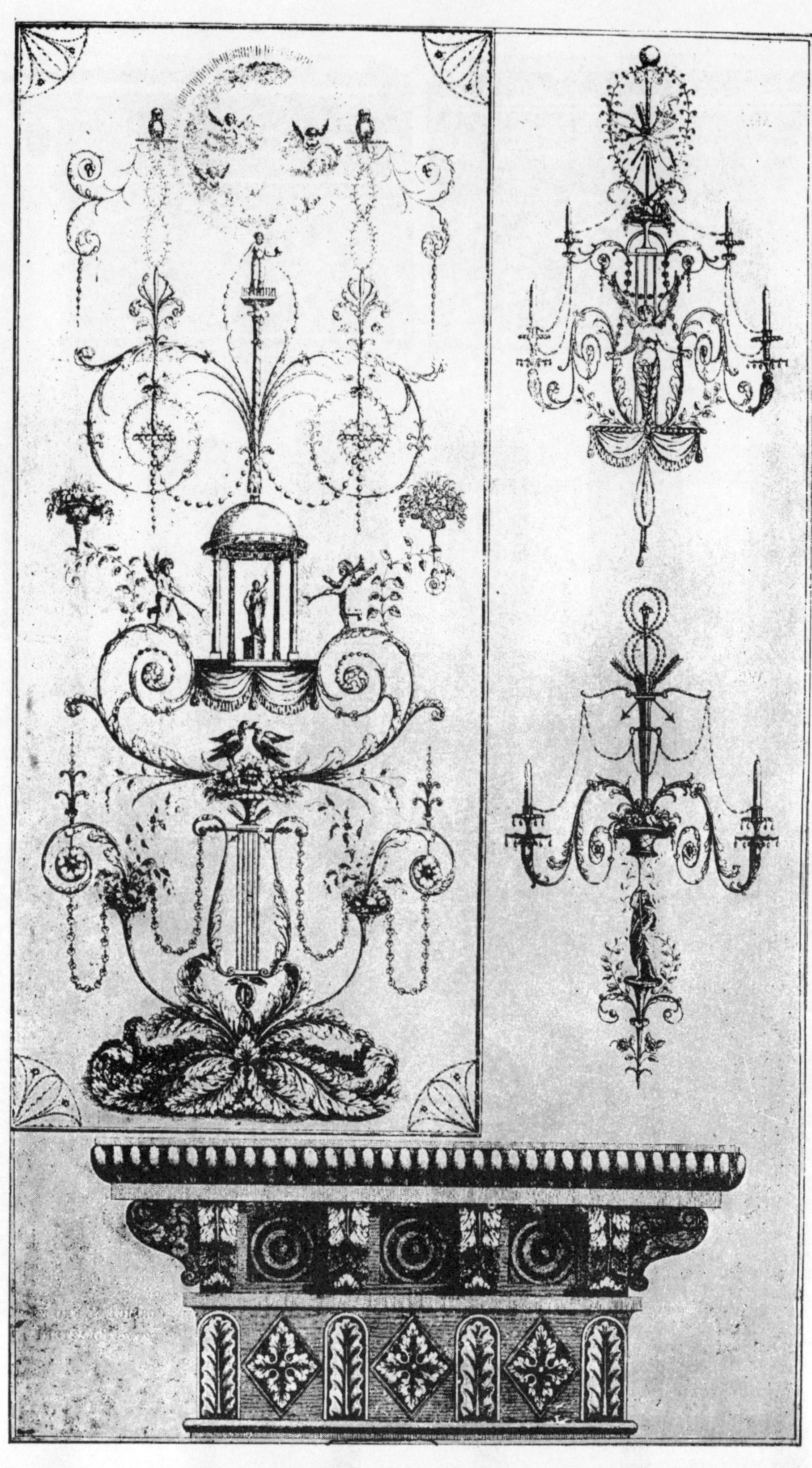

Ornament for a Painted Panel, Girandoles, and a Cornice and Frieze for a Pilaster

Ornament for a Frieze or Tablet

Pilasters for Commodes

SHERATON

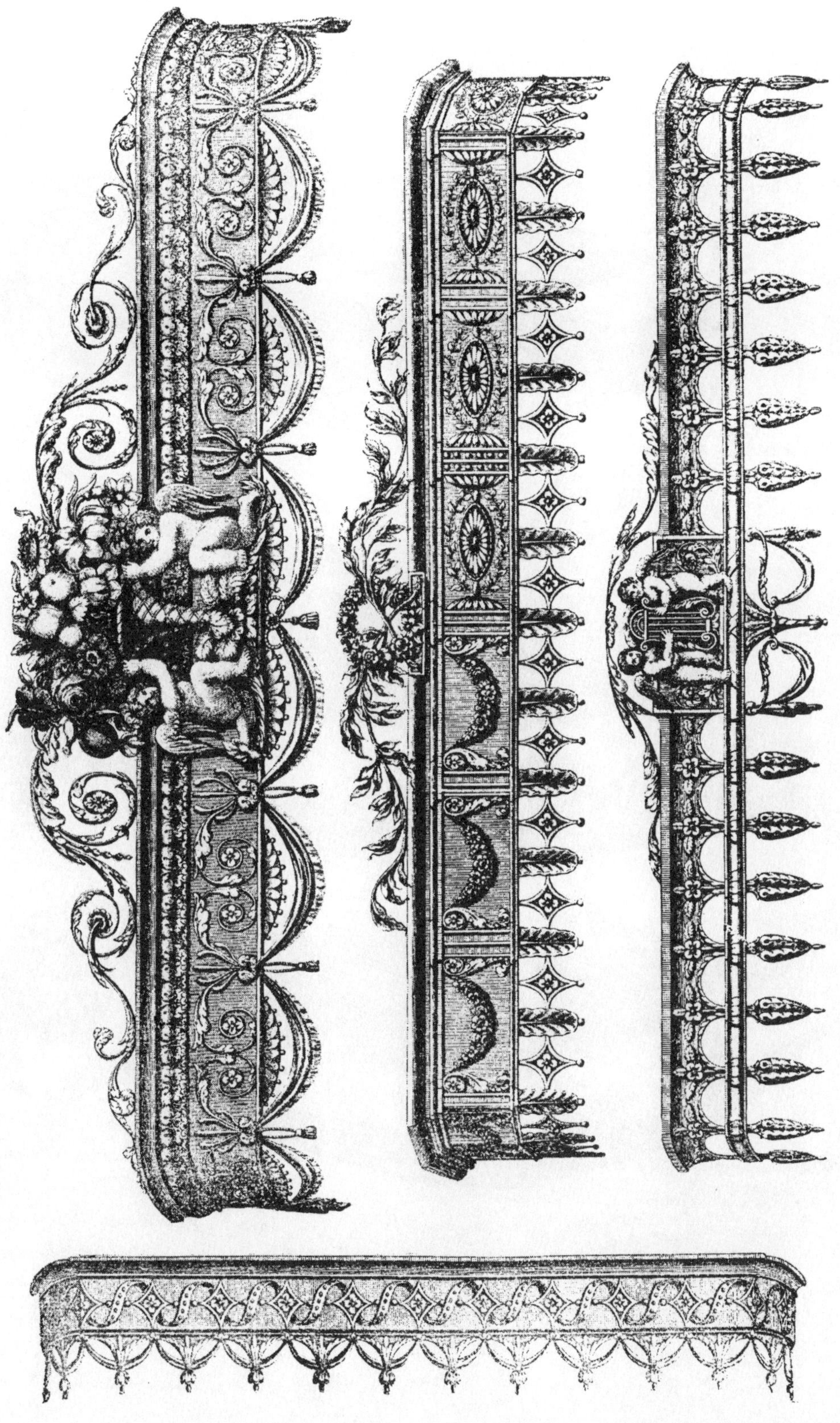

Window Cornices

Specimens of Ornament for the exercise of Learners

SHERATON

Pediments for Bookcases, and Centres for Pembroke Tables

A Dining Parlour, in imitation of the Prince of Wales's, a Pulpit, Tuscan Pedestal, Tuscan Entablature and Capital

THE FIVE ORDERS

Tuscan Doric Ionic Composite or Roman Corinthian

DESIGNS FOR HOUSEHOLD FURNITURE

DESIGNS

FOR

HOUSEHOLD FURNITURE

EXHIBITING A VARIETY OF

ELEGANT AND USEFUL PATTERNS

IN THE

Cabinet, Chair, and Upholstery Branches

ON EIGHTY-FOUR PLATES

BY THE LATE

T. SHERATON

CABINET-MAKER

SHERATON

Parlour Chairs

SHERATON

Parlour and Drawing-Room Chairs

SHERATON

Parlour and Drawing-Room Chairs

SHERATON

Herculaneums, Drawing-Room and Parlour Chairs

SHERATON

A Tub or Easy-Chair
A Cabriolet Arm-Chair
A Parlour Chair

Library Steps
Chair Bed

A Fauteuil Chair
A Hunting Chair
A Parlour Chair

SHERATON

Camp Chair Camp Table Bergère Chair
Masonic Chair Reading Chair
Nelson's Chairs

SHERATON

Corridor Chair, Conversation Chair, Curricules, and Grecian Sofa

Sofas

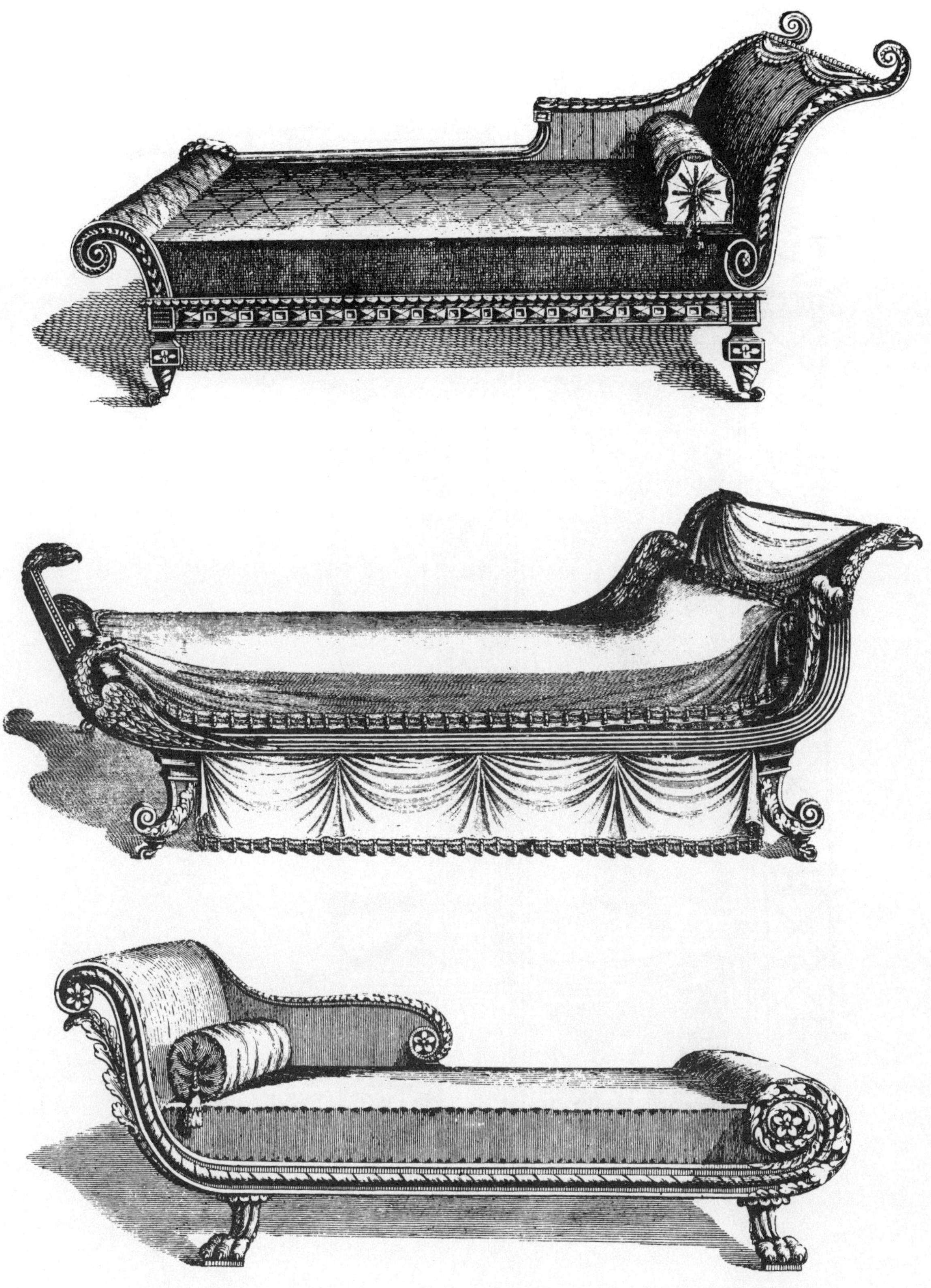

Grecian Couches

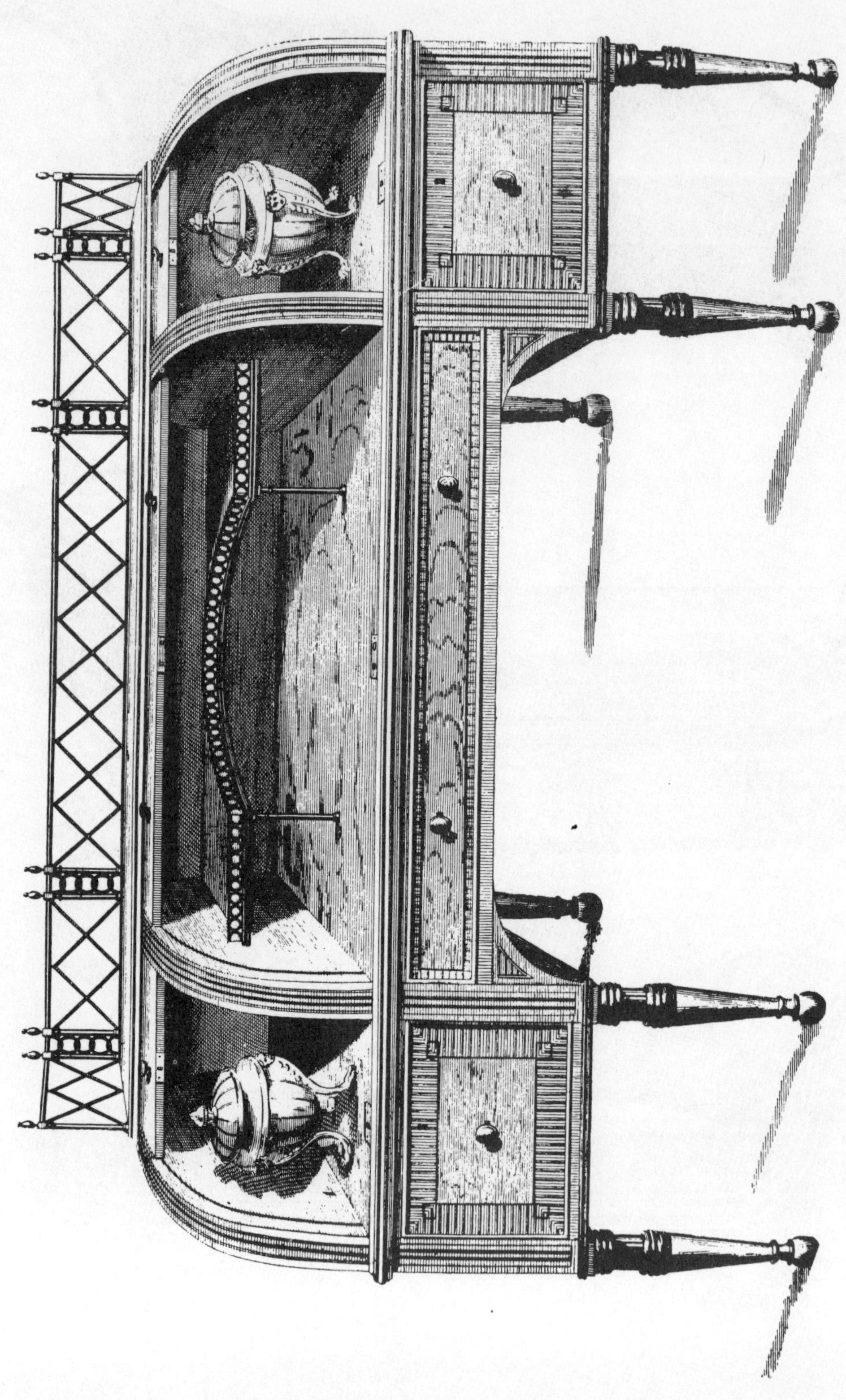

Sideboard

SHERATON

Side-Table and Sideboard

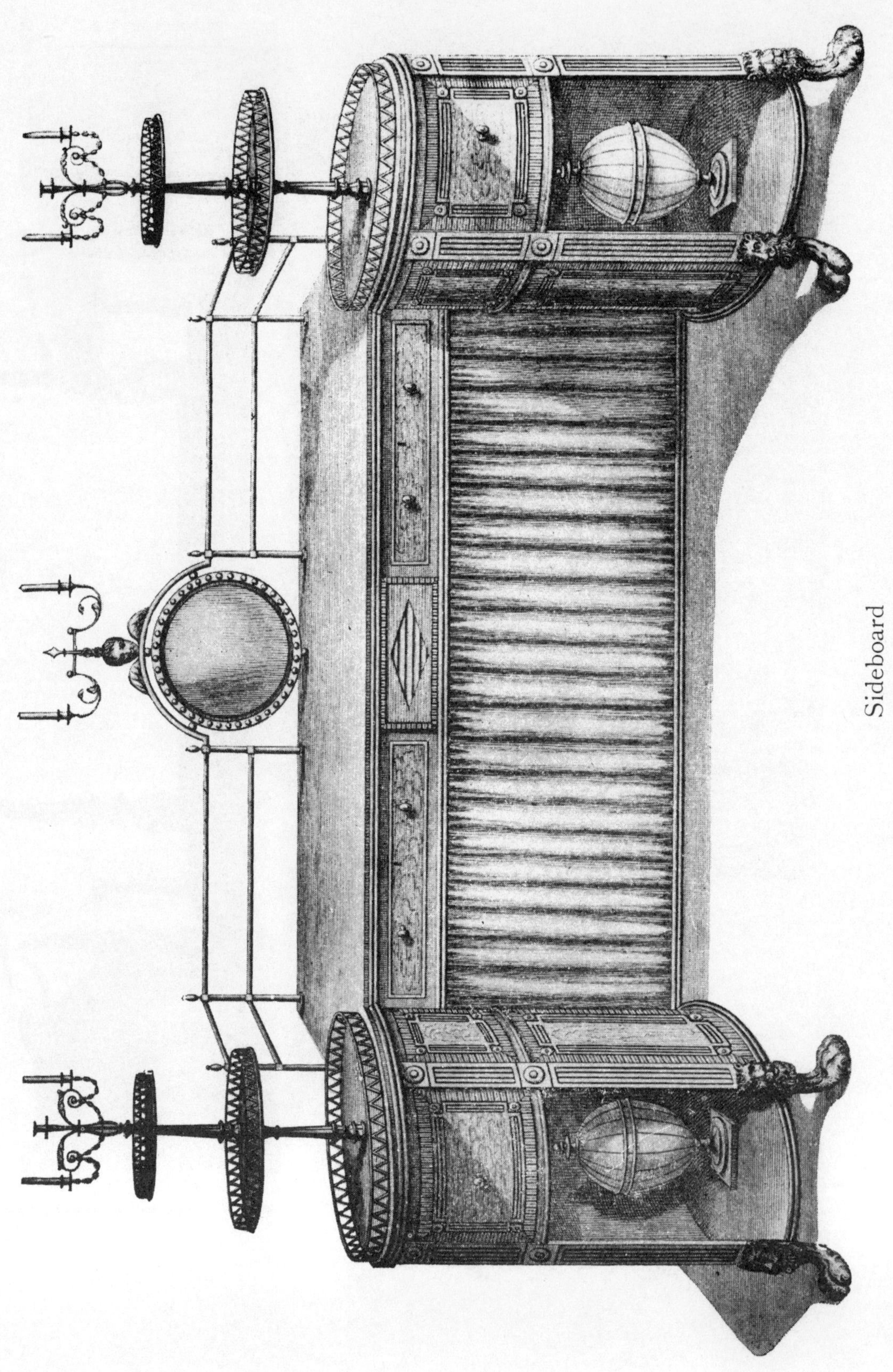

Sideboard

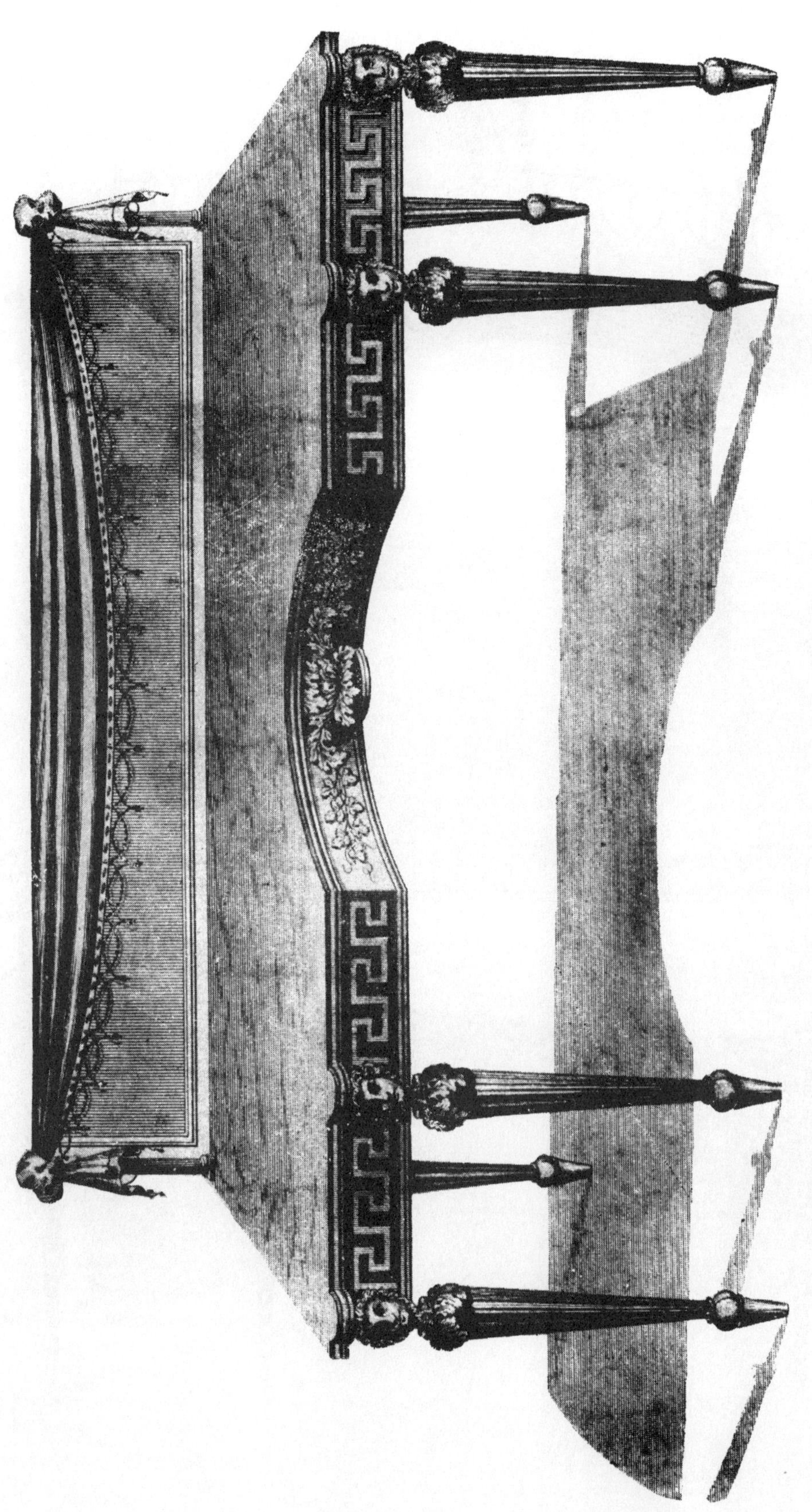

Side-Table

SHERATON

Side-Table and Sideboard

SHERATON

Pier Tables

A Commode and a Pier Table

SHERATON

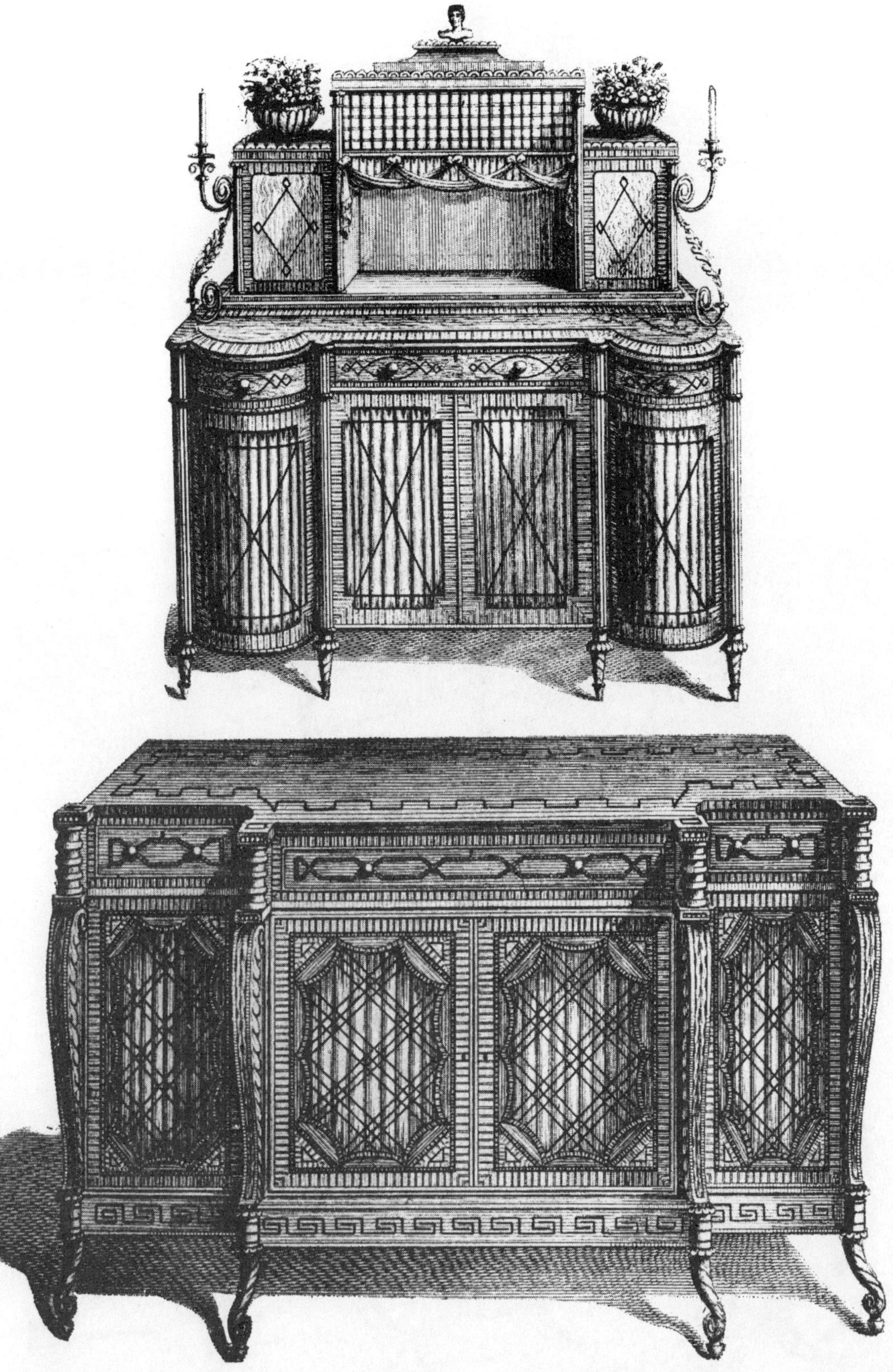

A Cabinet and a Commode

Cabinet and Quartetto Table

SHERATON

Lady's Writing and Dressing Table

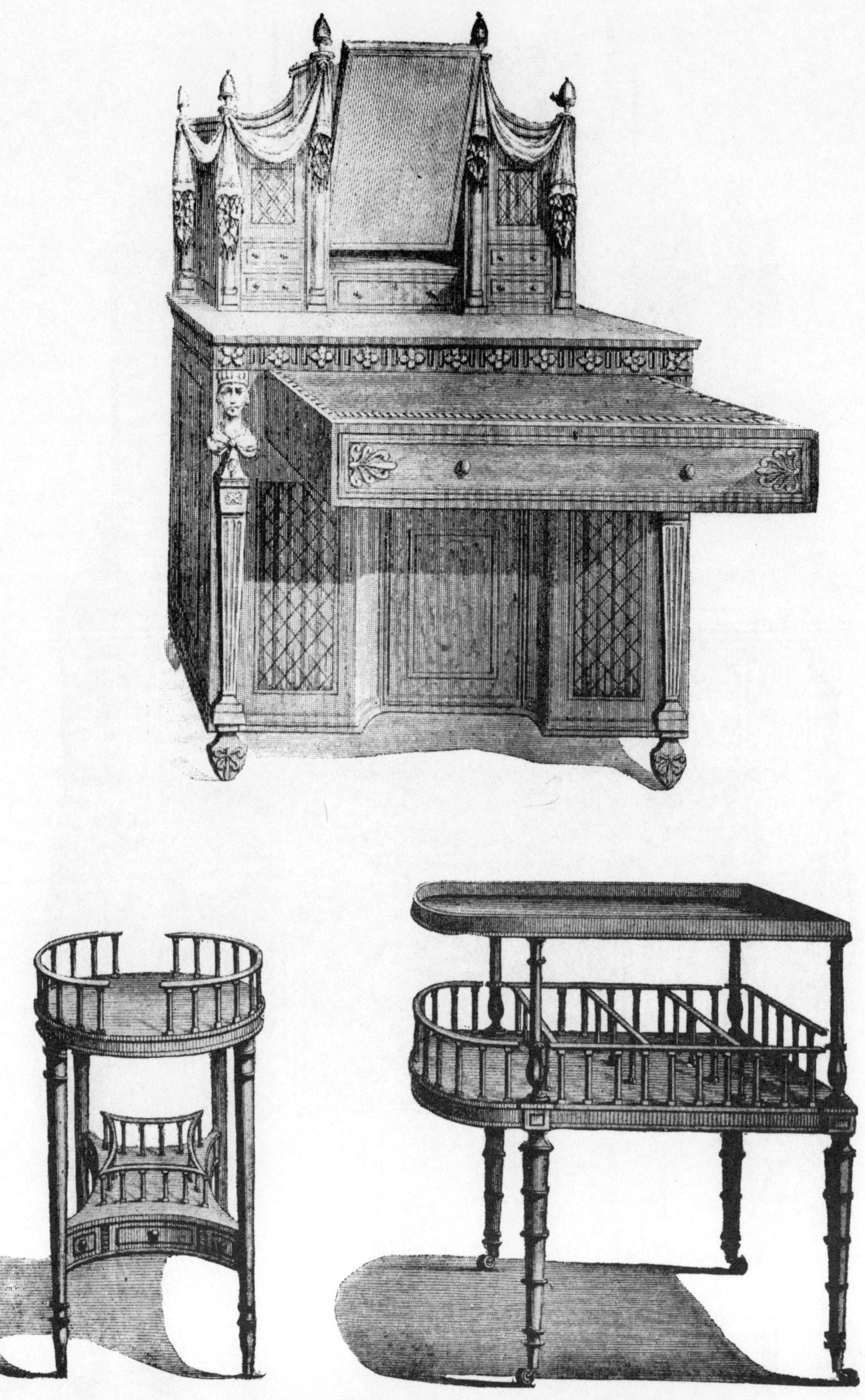

Lady's Writing and Dressing Table, and Dumb Waiters

SHERATON

Dressing Commode and Pier Table

SHERATON

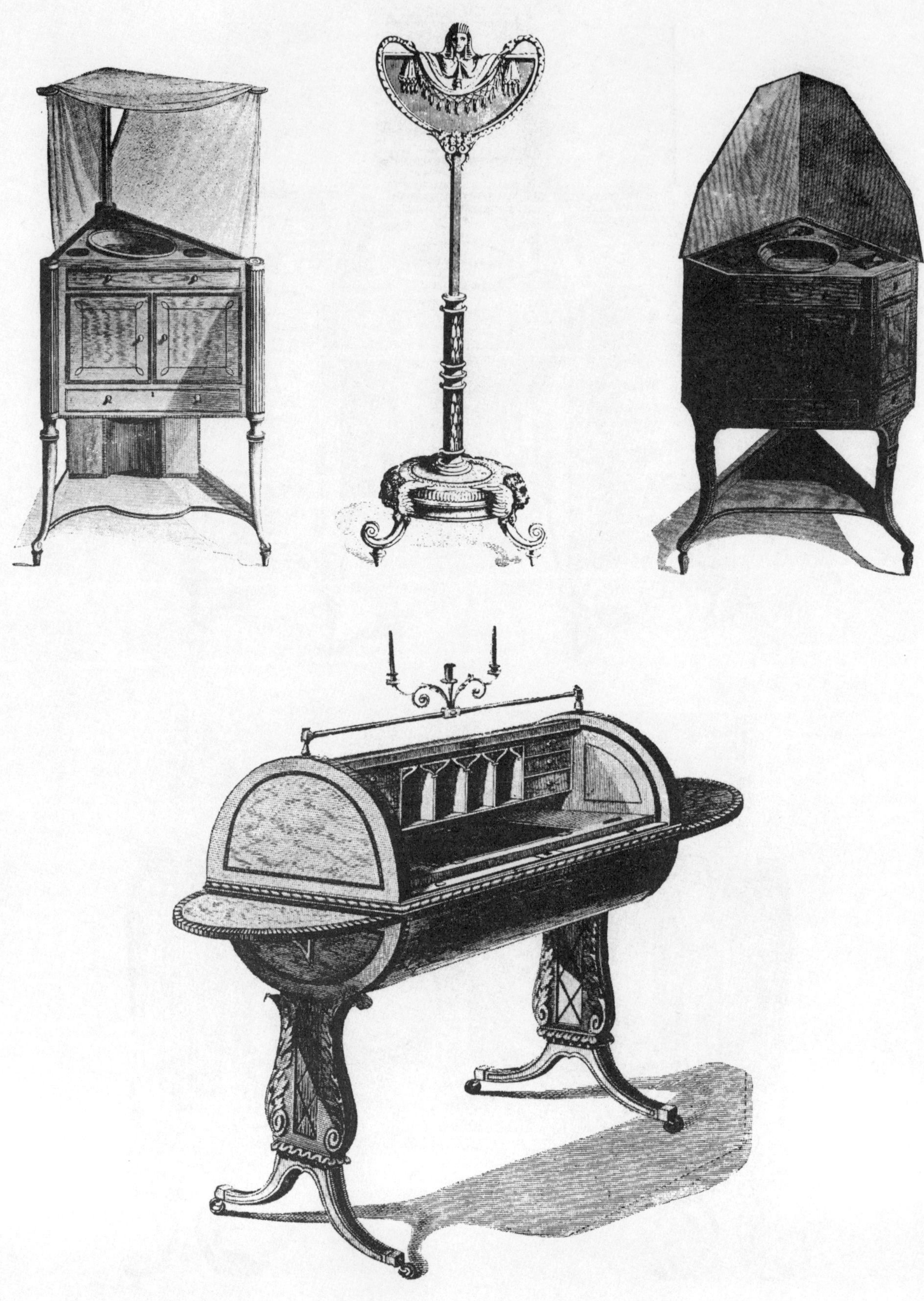

Corner Wash-hand Stand, Tripod Fire Screen, and Cylinder Writing Table

SHERATON

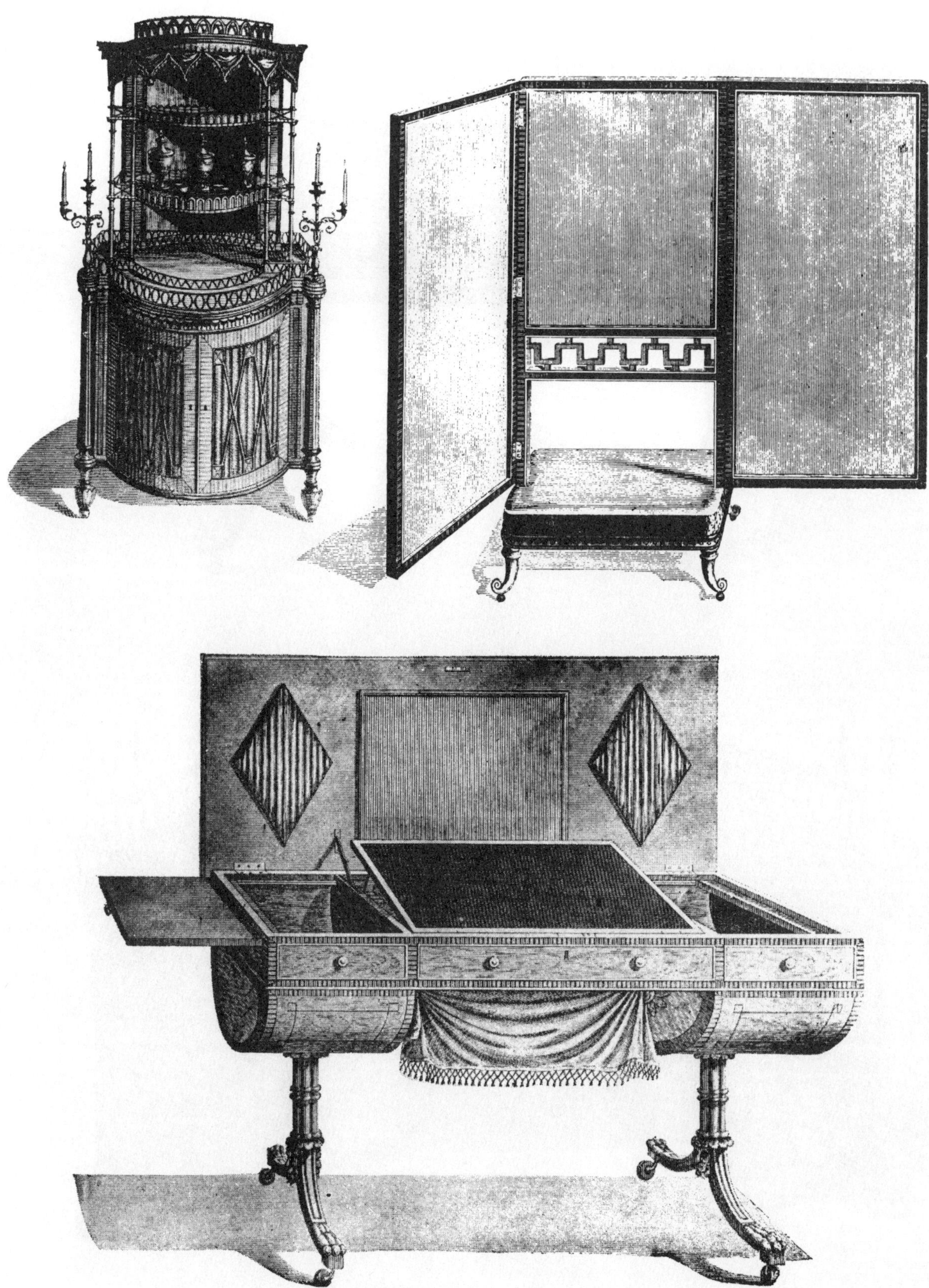

Buffet, Fire Screen, and Sofa Table

Sofa Table and Library Table

SHERATON

Loo Table and Sofa Table

SHERATON

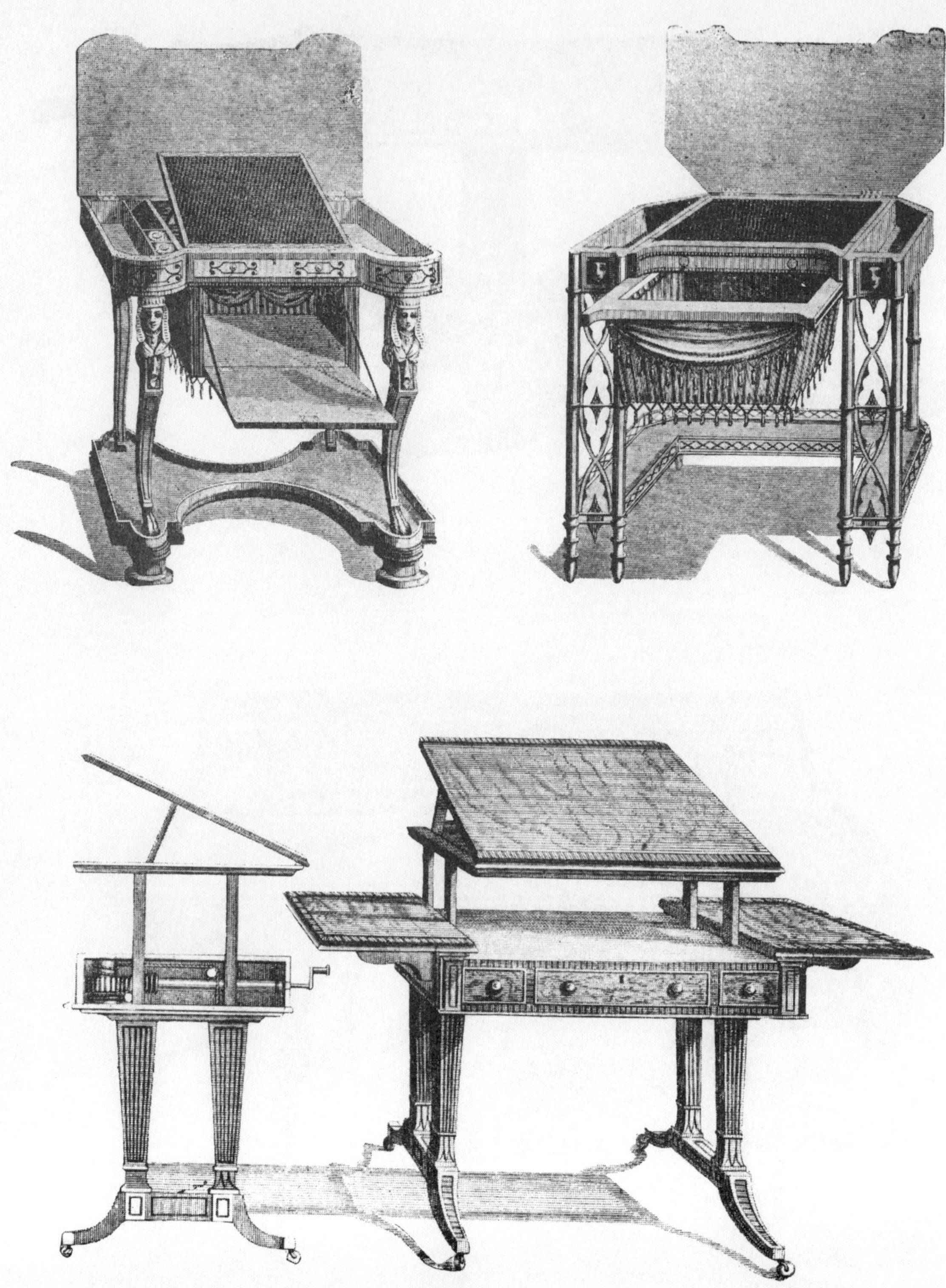

Ladies' Work Tables and Sofa Writing Table

Ladies' Work Tables and Pouch Tables

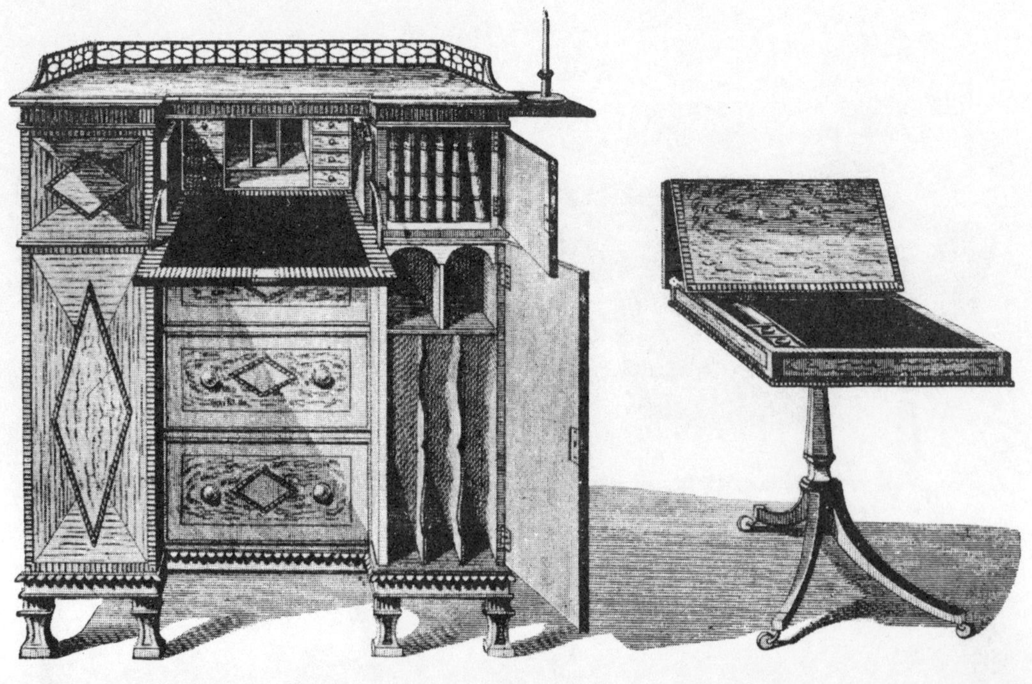

Dumb Waiters, Gentleman's Secretary, and Lady's Writing Table

SHERATON

Horseshoe Writing Table

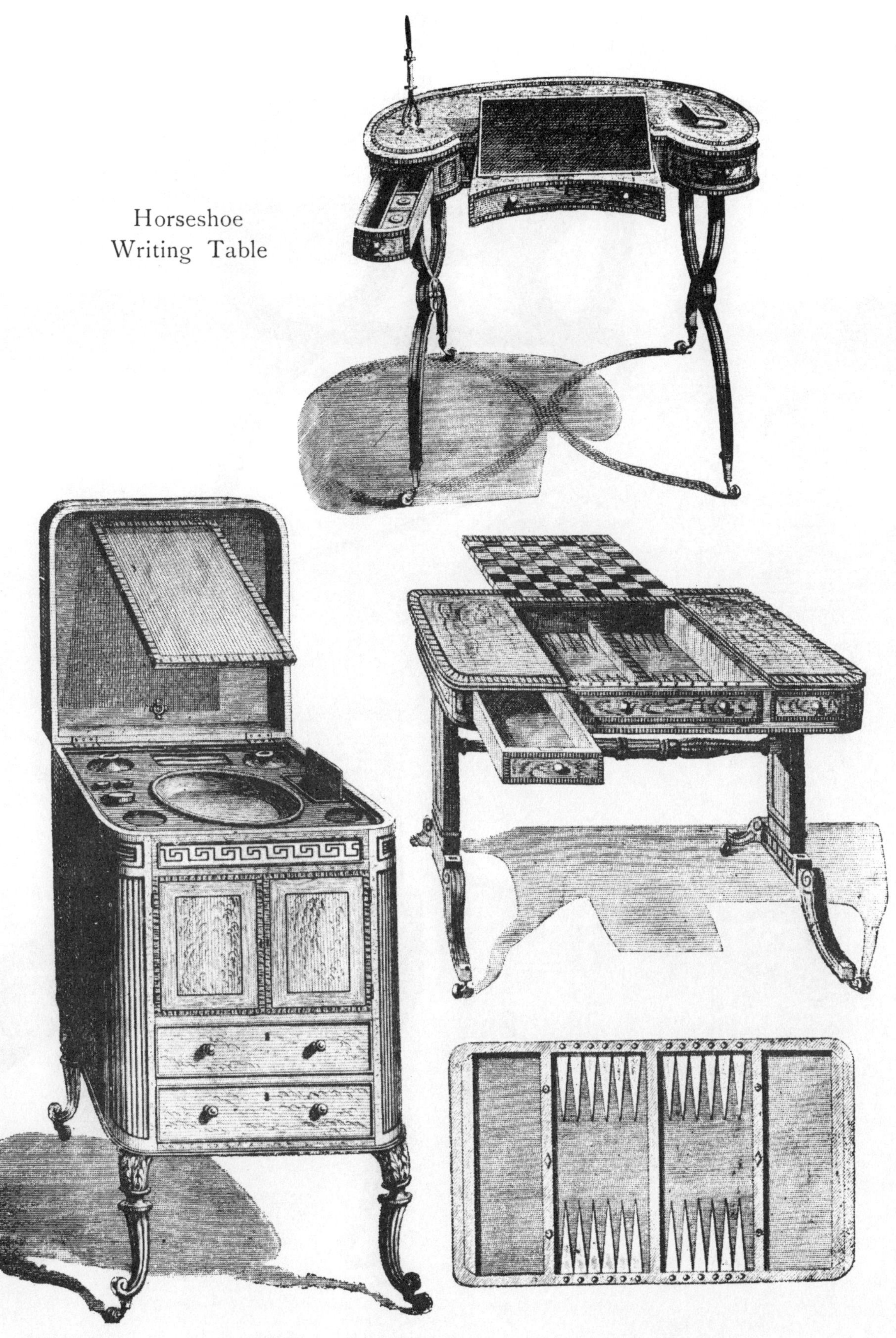

Gentleman's Shaving Table and Occasional Table

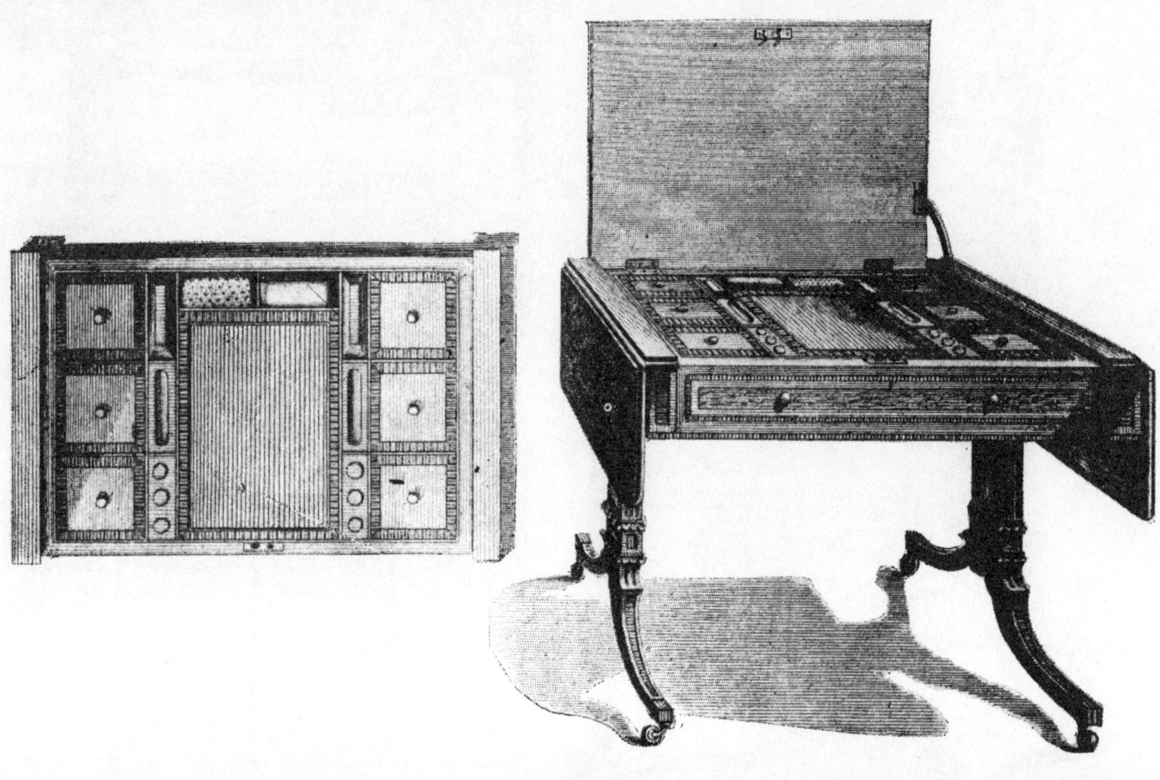

Pembroke Table, Dressing Table

SHERATON

Bureau Bookcase, Library Tables, and Moving Bookcase

Library Table

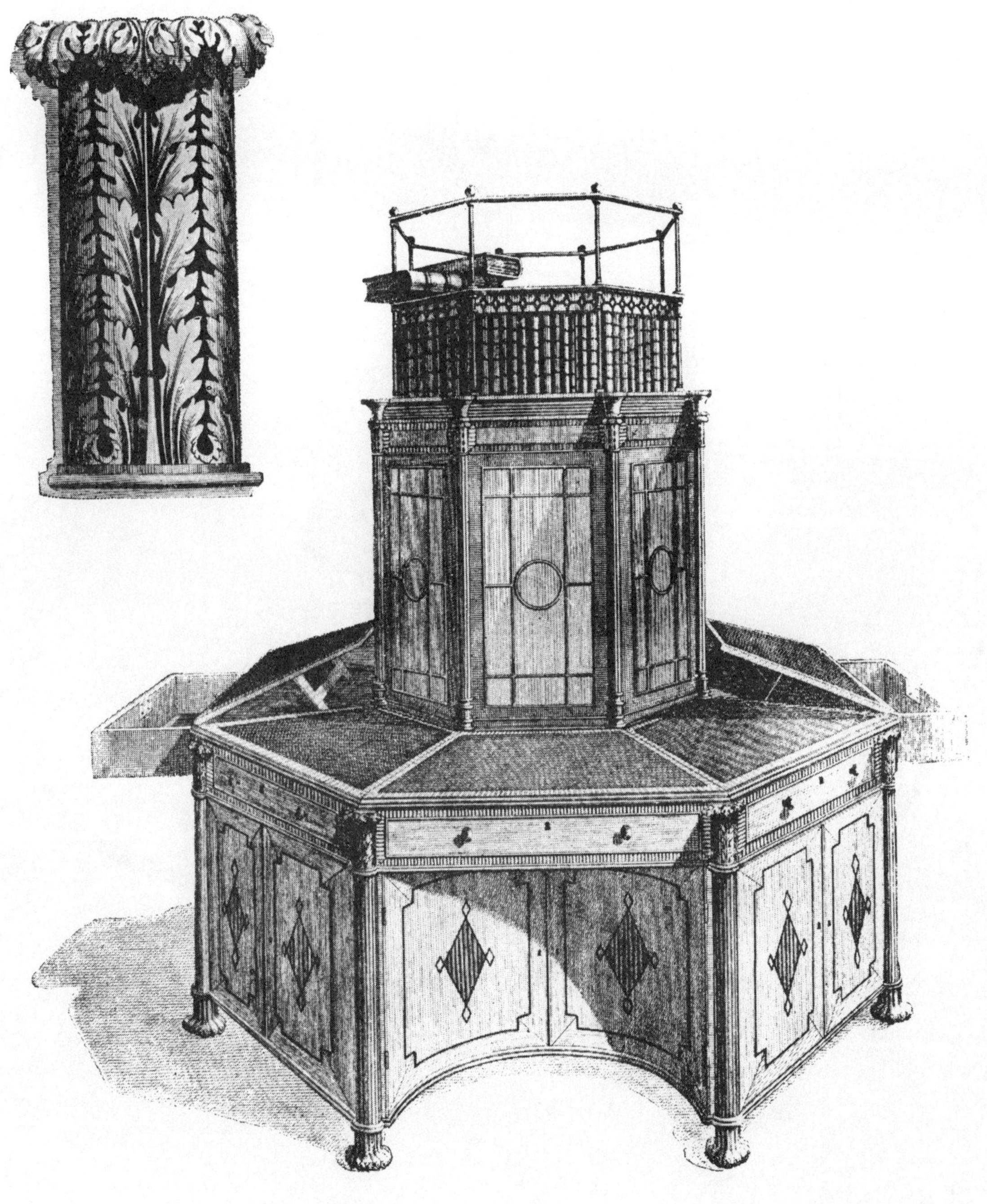

Octagon Library Table

New Design for a Dining Table

SHERATON

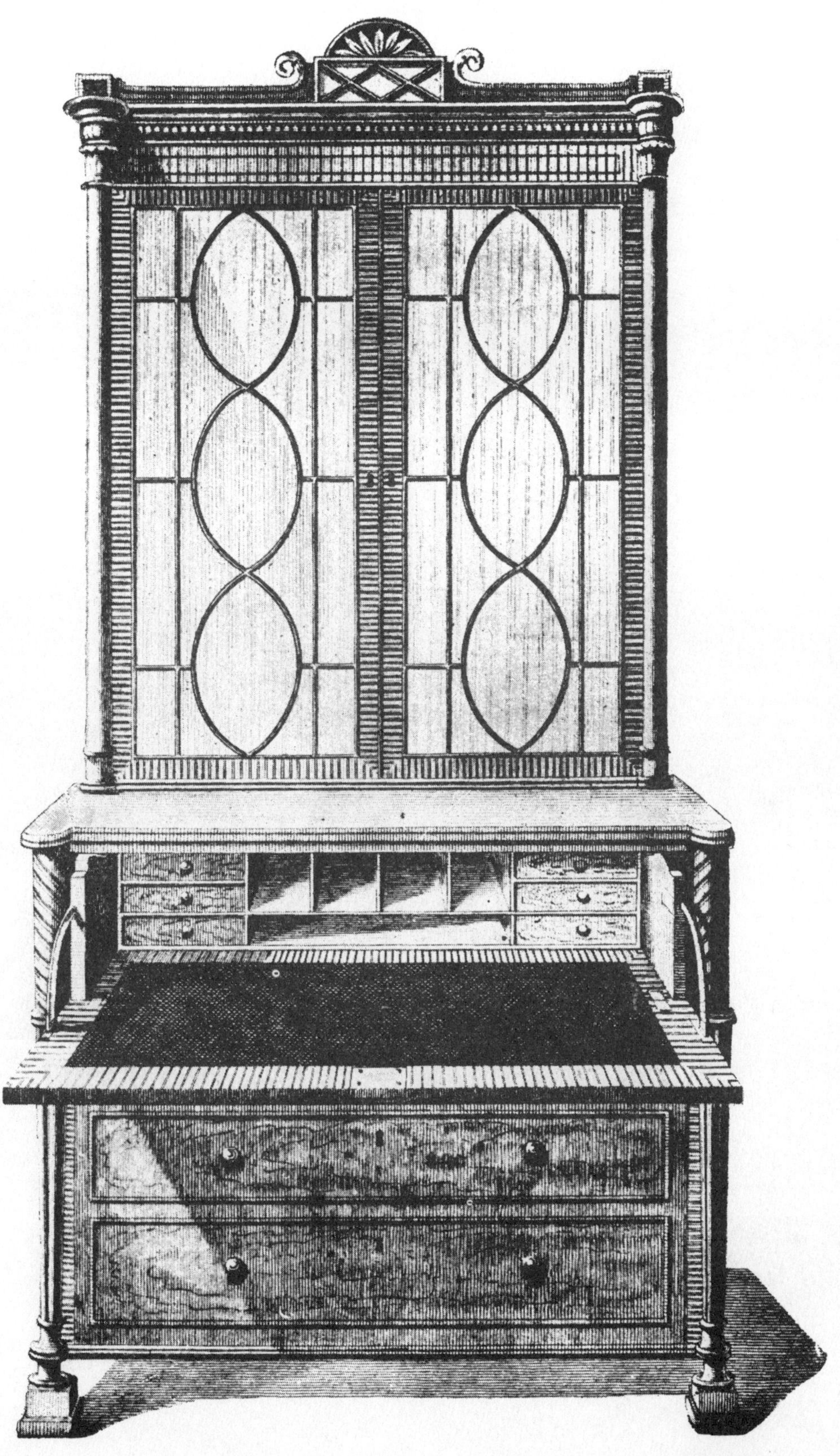

Secretary and Bookcase

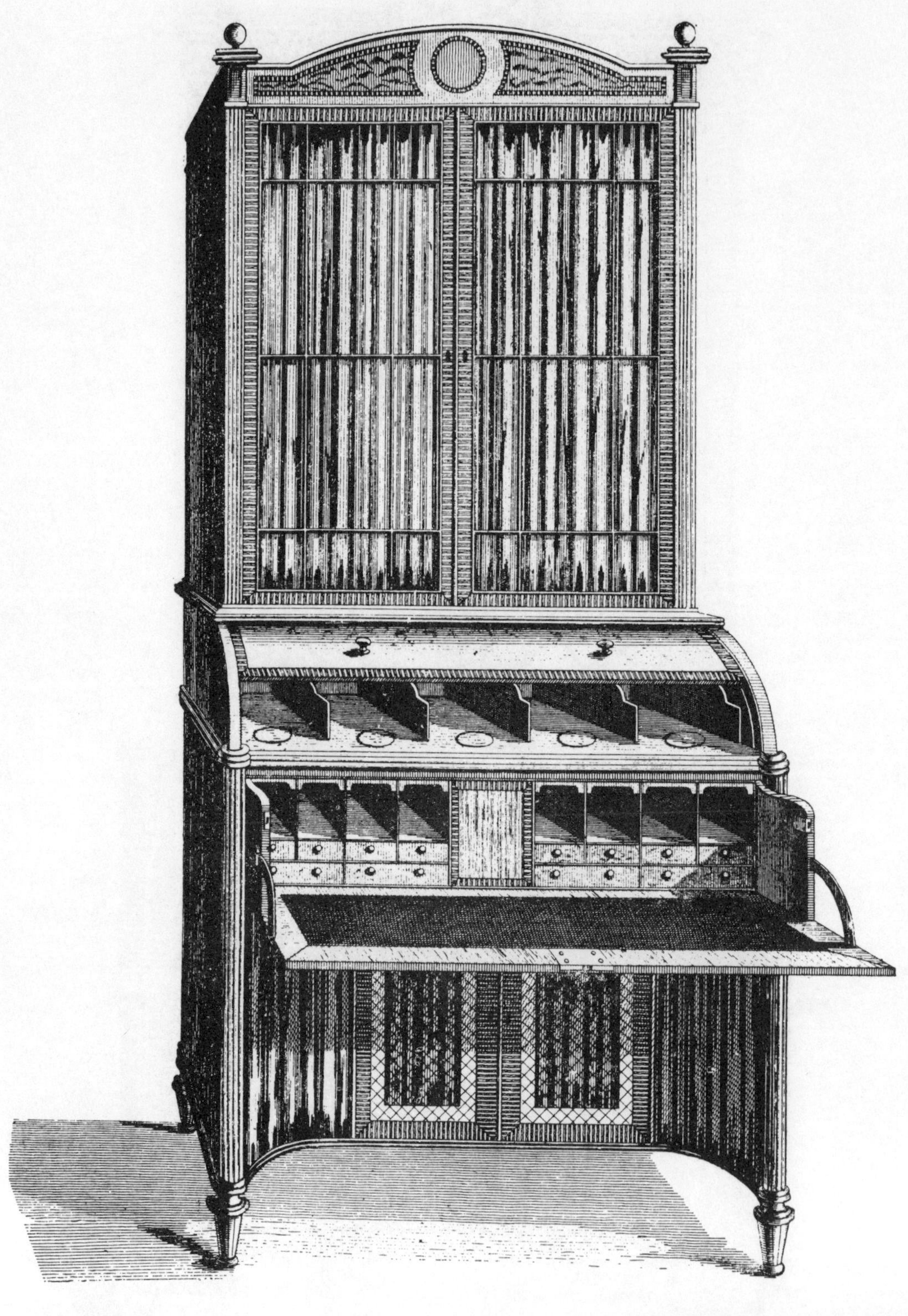

Secretary and Bookcase

SHERATON

Secretary and Bookcase

Bookcase

SHERATON

Bookcase

Bookcase

SHERATON

Cylinder Bookcase

SHERATON

Bookcase and Library-case

Sisters' Cylinder Bookcase

SHERATON

Bookcase Doors

SHERATON

Gothic Light

Chinese Light

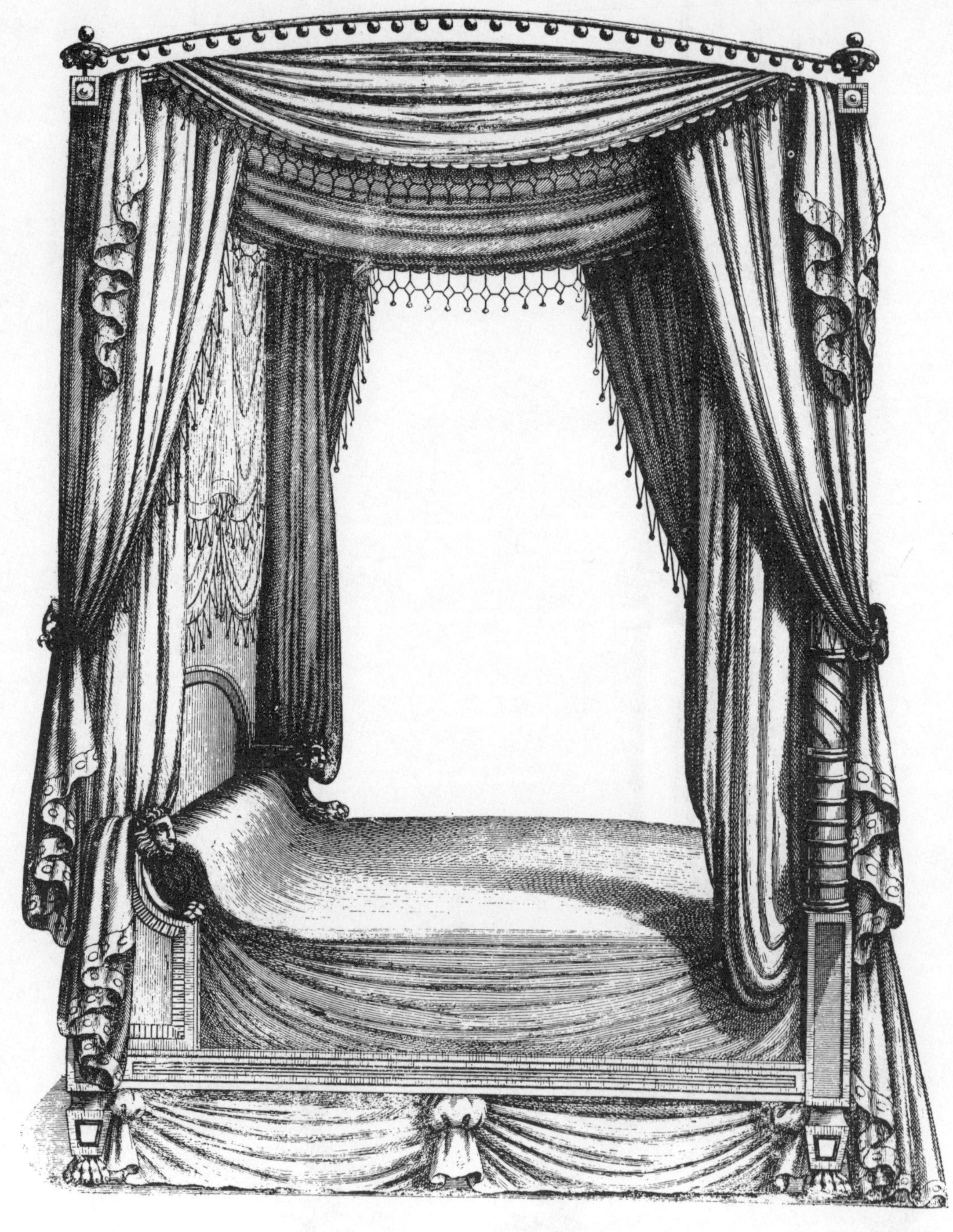

A New Design for a Bed

A New Design for a Bed

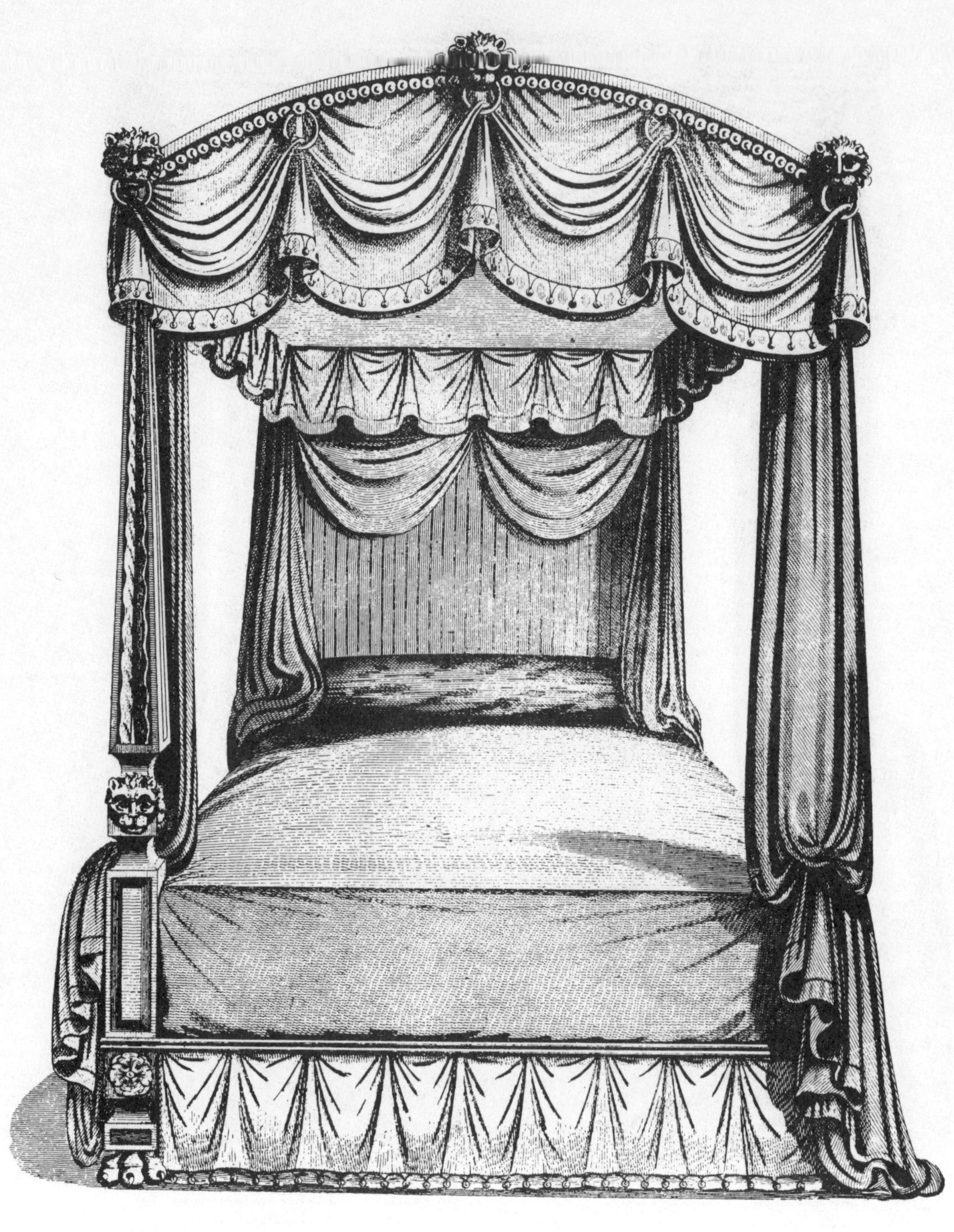

Design for a Bed

SHERATON

Design for a Bed

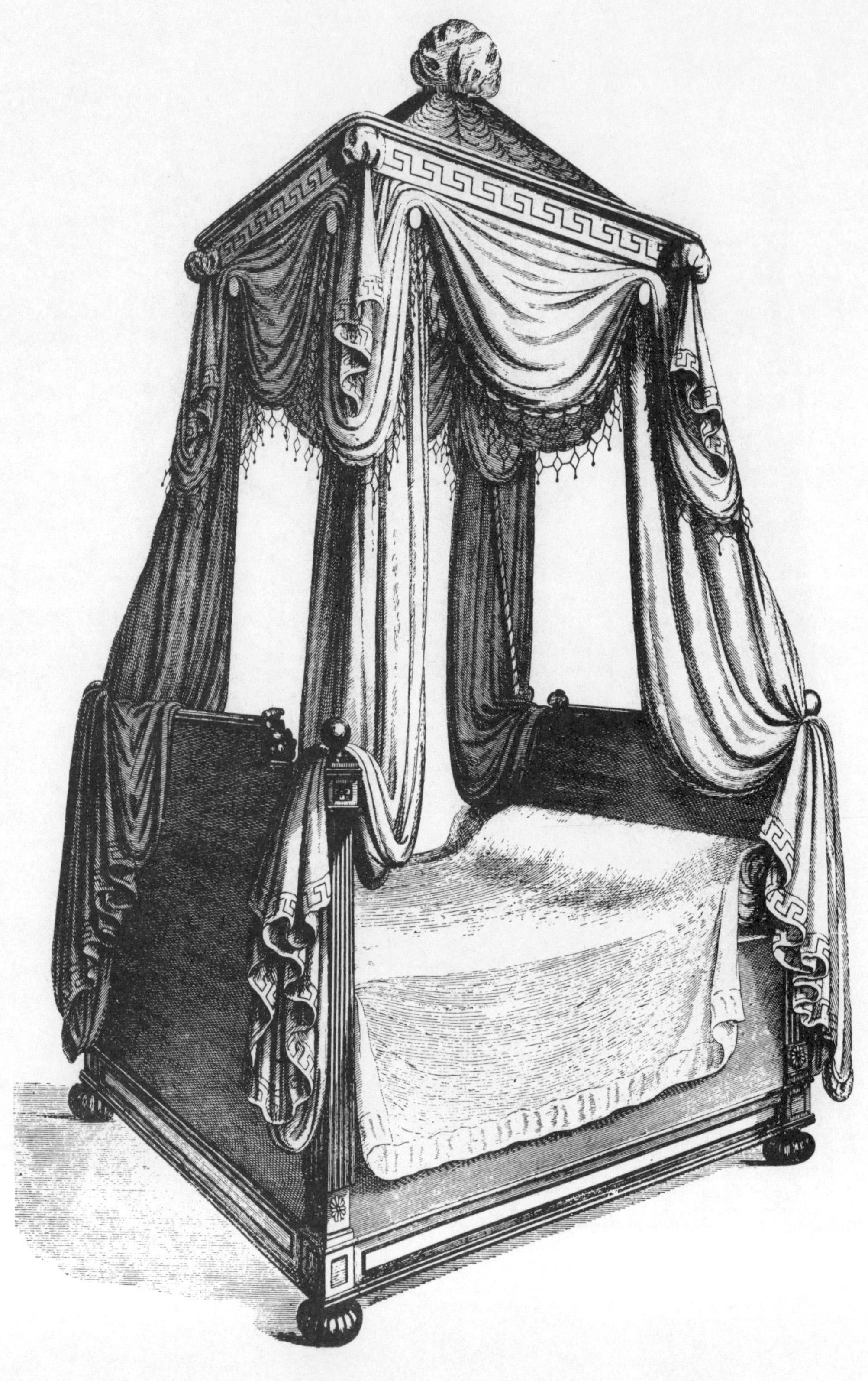

French Bed

SHERATON

French Bed

A Grecian Bed

Alcove Bed

Canopy Bed

Canopy Bed

State Bed

SHERATON

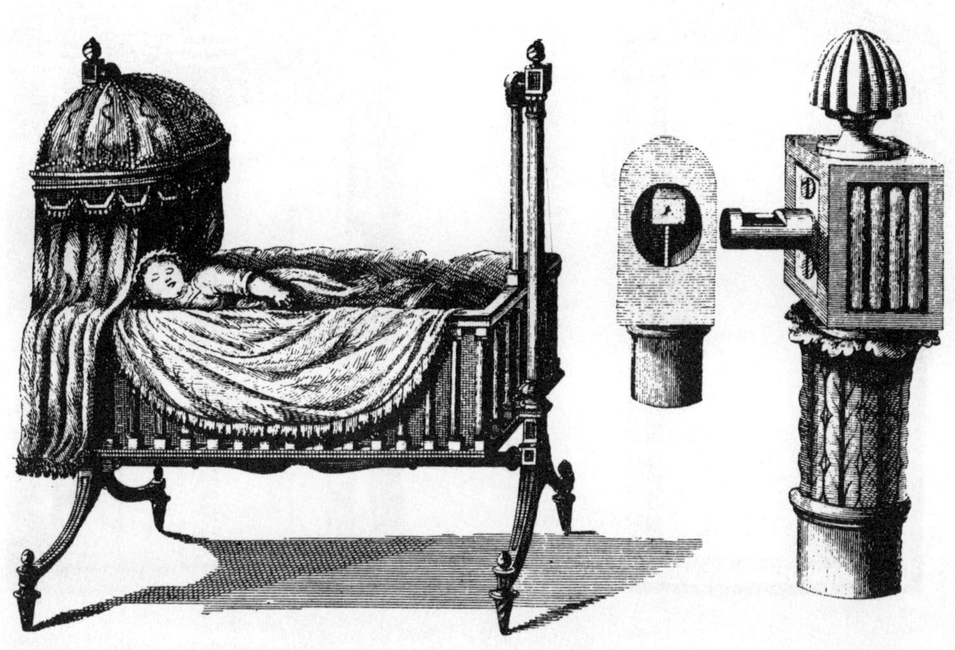

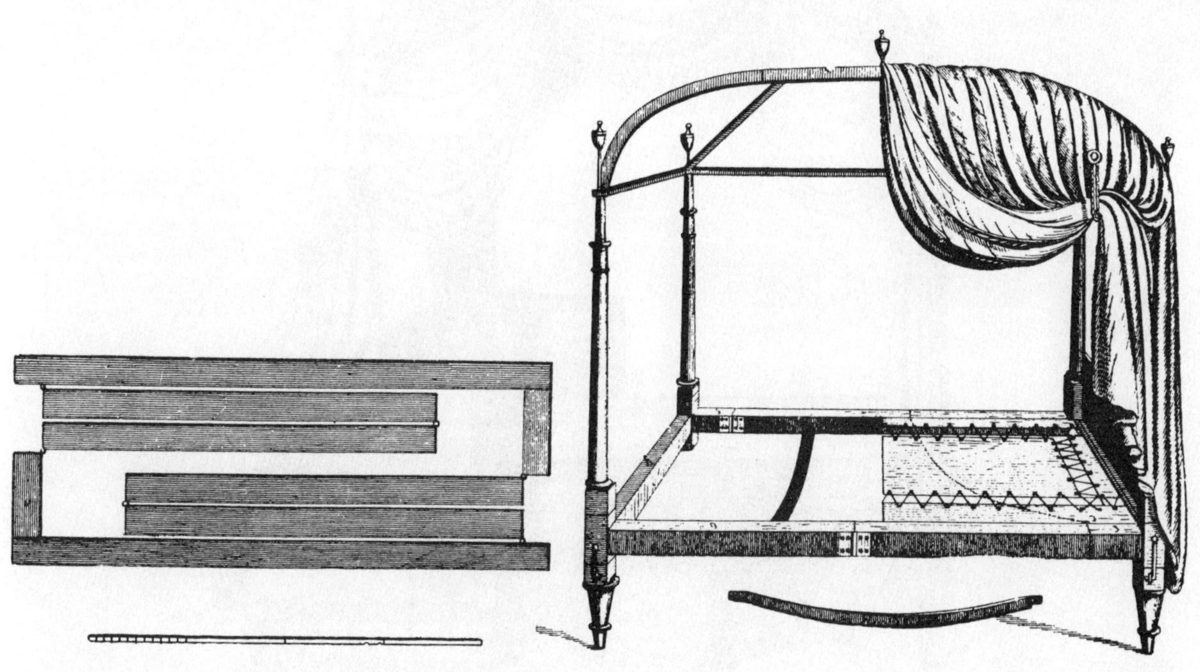

A Swinging Crib Bed   Camp Bed

Window and Pier Glass Draperies, and Sofa-Bed

SHERATON

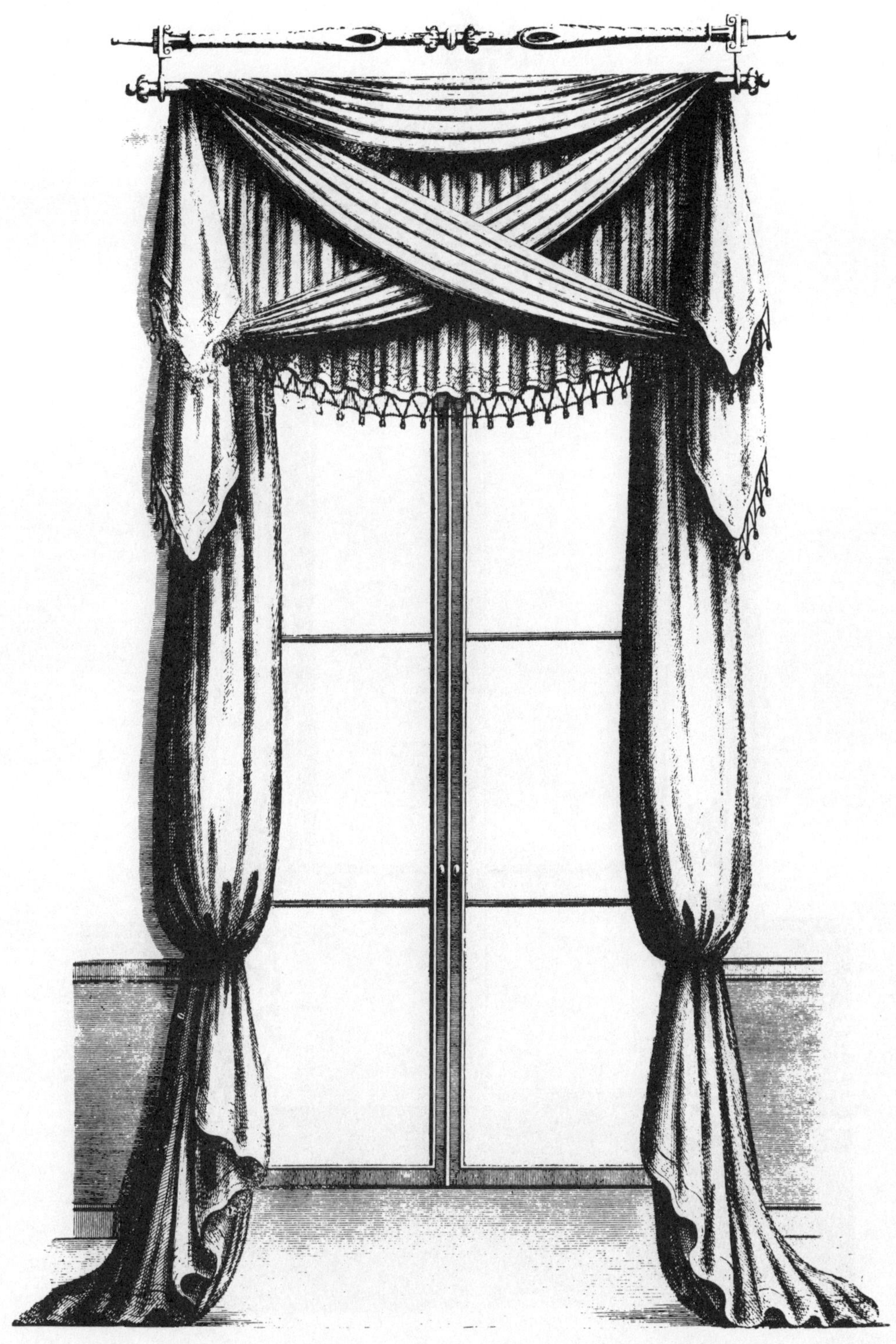

Window Draperies

Window Draperies

SHERATON

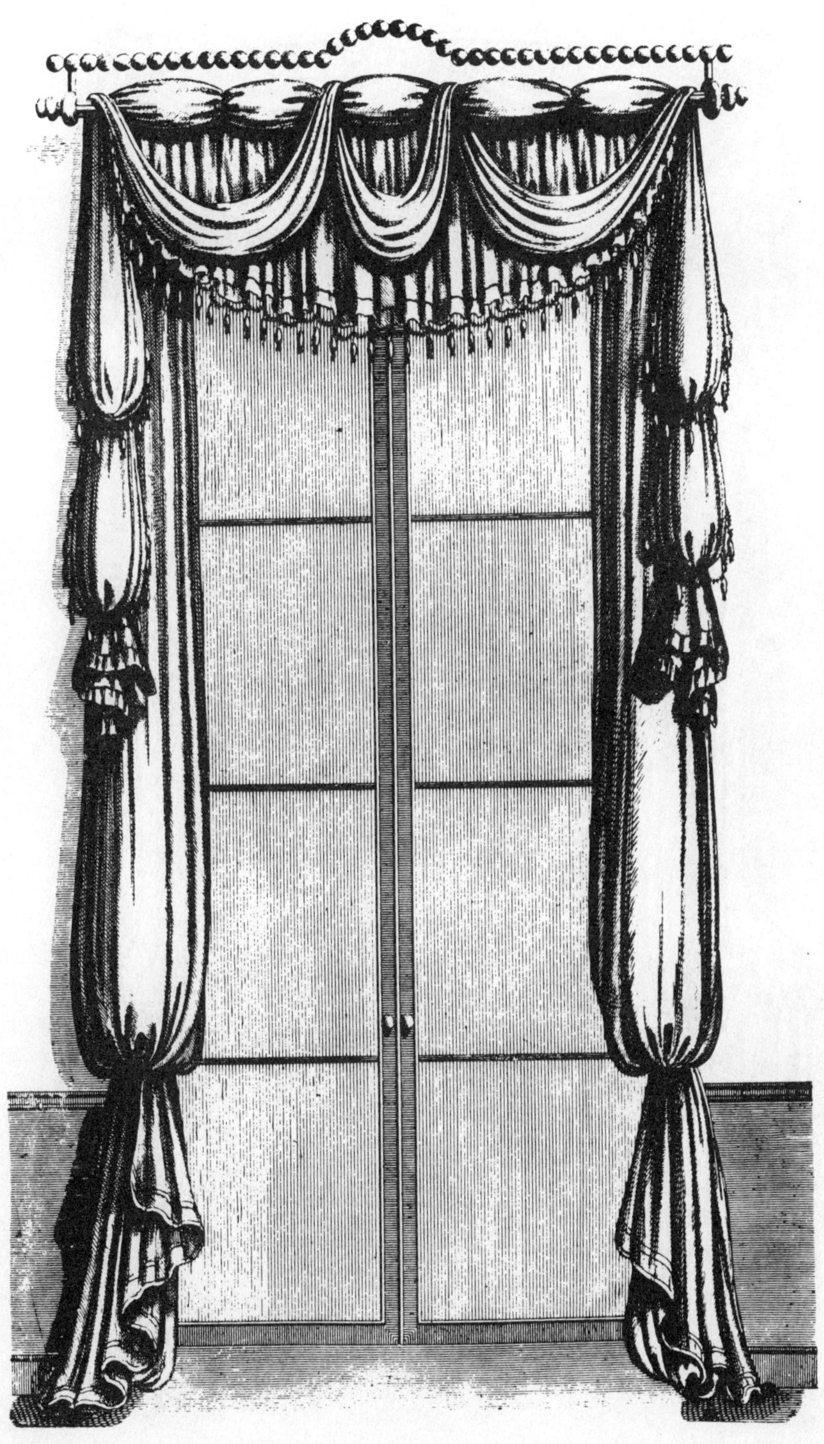

New Window Draperies

New French Window Draperies

SHERATON

Window Draperies

Window Drapery and Drawing-Room Chair

SHERATON

Window Drapery

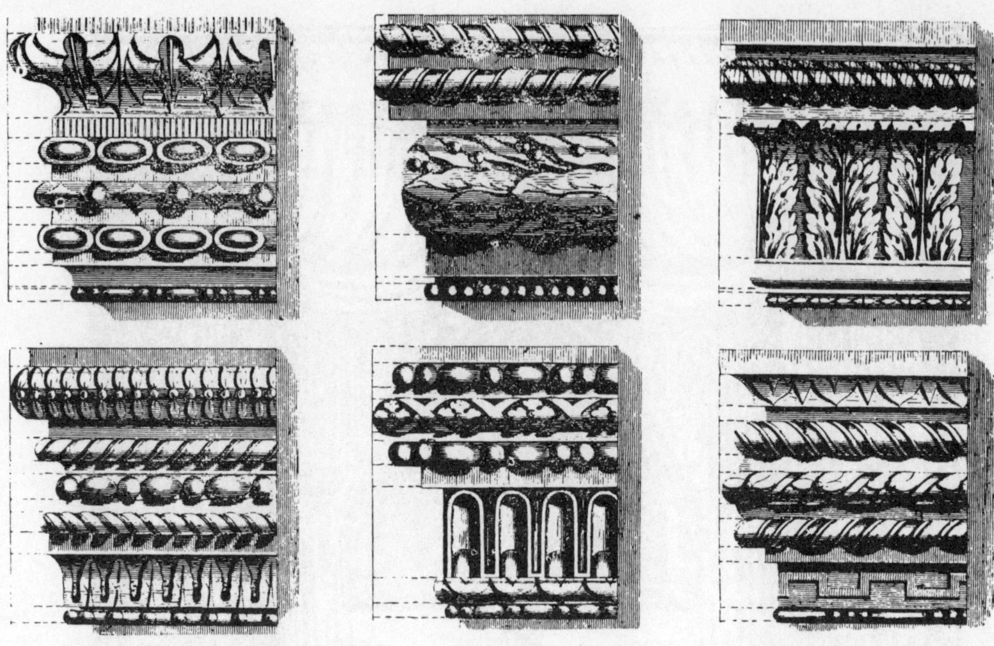

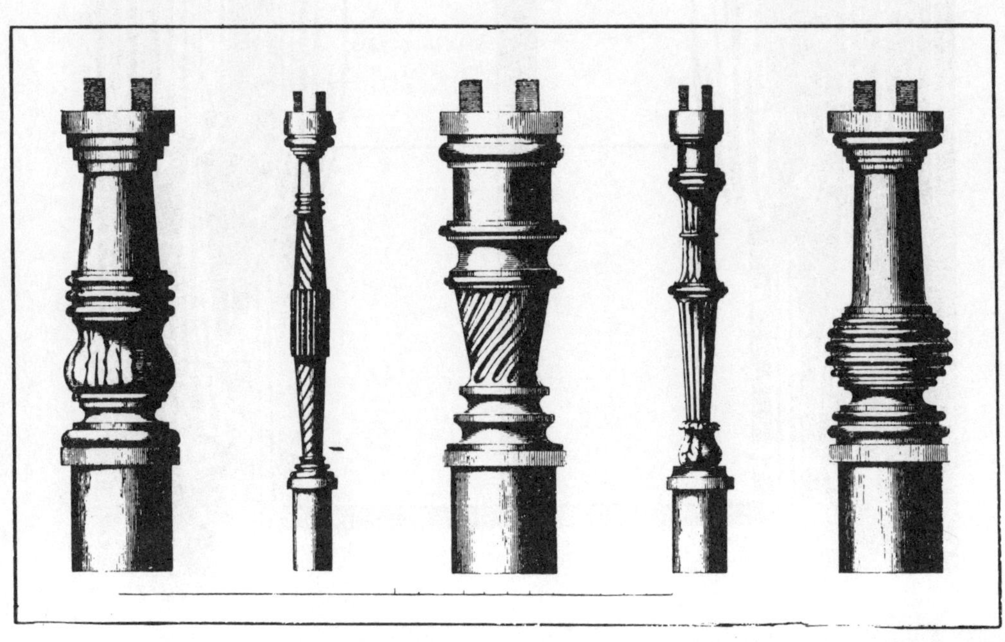

Mouldings for Architraves and Window Cornices, and Pillars for Tables